Android®

Fully Loaded,

Second Edition

Rob Huddleston

WILEY

Wiley Publishing, Inc.

Android® Fully Loaded, Second Edition

Published by:
Wiley Publishing, Inc.
111 River Street
Hoboken, NJ 07030-5774
www.wiley.com

Published by Wiley Publishing, Inc., Indianapolis, Indiana
Published simultaneously in Canada

ISBN: 978-1-118-17302-2

Manufactured in the United States of America

10 9 8 7 6 5 4 3 2 1

For general information on our other products and services or to obtain technical support, please contact our Customer Care department within the U.S. at (800) 762-2974, outside the U.S. at (317) 572-3993 or fax (317) 572-4002.

Wiley also publishes its books in a variety of electronic formats. Some content that appears in print may not be available in electronic books. For more information about Wiley products, please visit our web site at www.wiley.com.

Library of Congress Control Number: 2011945007

Acknowledgments

Thank you to Stephanie McComb, Acquisitions Editor at Wiley, for entrusting yet another edition of this book to me. This marks the fourth project we have worked on together, and I look forward to many more to come.

Thank you also to my fantastic agent Margot Hutchison for handling all of the business details so that I don't have to.

Thank you to Chris Pichereau, David Sechrist, Debbie Abshier, and all of the others at Abshier House for their hard work shepherding this project along, keeping me on track, and making sure my English makes sense.

Thank you to Phil Nickinson, who once again agreed to be my tech editor. Phil is the editor of AndroidCentral.com, one of the foremost experts on all things Android, and a great cousin. Neither this or the prior version would have been possible without him.

Finally, thank you to Kelley, Jessica, and Xander. I love you all.

Credits

Senior Acquisitions Editor
Stephanie McComb

Editorial Director
Robyn B. Siesky

**Vice President &
Executive Group Publisher**
Richard Swadley

**Vice President &
Executive Publisher**
Barry Pruett

Business Manager
Amy Knies

Marketing Manager
Sandy Smith

**Production Editor, Copy Editing,
Layout, Design, Proofreading,
and Indexing**
Abshier House

Technical Editor
Phil Nickinson

Cover Image
Michael E. Trent

About the Author

Rob Huddleston is an Adjunct Professor at the Art Institute of California, Sacramento in the Web Design and Interactive Media department, where he teaches programming and design, focusing heavily on mobile development. He has been creating web pages and applications since 1994, and worked for many years as a corporate trainer, where he taught web and graphic design to thousands of students from all walks of life.

Rob is the author of *XML: Your visual blueprint™* for building expert websites using XML, CSS, XHTML; HTML, XHTML; and *CSS: Your visual blueprint™* for designing effective websites; *Master VISUALLY: Dreamweaver CS4* and *Flash Professional CS4; ActionScript 3: Your visual blueprint™* for creating interactive projects in Flash CS4 Professional; the *Adobe Flash Catalyst Bible; Teach Yourself VISUALLY Web Design,* and the first edition of this book.

When he is not writing or teaching, Rob hangs out with his wife and two children, runs the Sacramento Adobe Users Group, sees a ridiculous number of movies, and obsesses about Firefly and Serenity.

You can contact Rob via his website at http://www.robhuddleston.com or follow him on Twitter at http://twitter.com/robhuddles.

Contents

Introduction

Consider this, four short years ago, very few people had ever heard the term "smartphone." While the term is in fact quite a bit older — according to Wikipedia, it was first applied to the Ericsson GS88 in 1997 — it was not until Steve Jobs announced the first iPhone in 2007 that the term entered common usage. The smartphone almost perfectly fits the definition of a disruptive technology; that is, one of those technologies that comes along every so often that radically changes our world. One simple example: Smartphones have created a massive shift in how we interact online. Today, most people visiting the top sites on the web still use desktop and laptop computers, but that trend is quickly changing. In fact, estimates are that by 2015, smartphones will surpass traditional computers to become the primary means by which we get online.

The smartphone market itself is changing so fast it is hard to keep up. At times it seems like new devices are released almost every day. Desktop PC users are used to hearing about new versions of Windows or the Macintosh operating system every three or four years, while their devices seem to get new versions at a breakneck speed.

Apple led the next revolution in mobile devices in 2010 with the announcement of the iPad. Just as smartphones existed before the iPhone, tablets existed before the iPad, but it was the device that brought the idea of tablets into the mainstream.

On both the phone and the tablet market, Google's Android was the latecomer. The first Android phone was released in September 2008, almost 20 months after the iPhone was unveiled. The iPad preceded commercially viable Android tablets by more than six months.

Despite that, Android market share has exploded. A 2011 report by research firm Nielsen showed that Android was the number one mobile operating system, with 40 percent of smartphone users on the platform, compared to 28 percent on Apple's iOS. The report did not look at tablets, but while most anaylists agree that the iPad still dominates the market, it is a dominance unlikely to persist.

These new mobile technologies have also opened up a new world for developers, providing an exciting and rapidly expanding market for applications built for mobile devices, which in turn provides you, the end user, a seemingly limitless supply of apps that will increase your productivity by enabling you to check e-mail, read and edit documents, view presentations, and much more — all on your device. At least as many apps exist to decrease your productivity as well: No shortage of games exist to allow you to kill time and drain your battery while having fun.

I assume you are buying this book because you recently bought an Android-based, whether it be a smartphone or a tablet. You hold in your hand a miniature computer; a computer so far advanced from those that took us to the moon that it is almost unfair to label both with that same term, computer. In some ways, carrying a device with that kind of speed and capabilities can be a bit daunting. Hopefully, reading through this book will help strip away some of that mystery, will help you better understand your new device, and will enable you to truly leverage all that it can do.

Most of all, please enjoy your new device.

PART I

The Basics

Android Basics

The Skim

Had someone told me five years ago that I would be spending more time, and getting more done, on my mobile phone than on my laptop, I would have laughed. For years, I was resistant to the changes happening in the mobile space. I had a cellphone, of course, but it was basic: one of those weird models whose primary function was making phone calls. I did not figure that I needed a camera in my phone, because after all I had a very nice camera when I wanted to take pictures. In fact, the only reason my next cell phone had a camera was because by that point, they simply did not make phones without cameras anymore.

That all changed in 2008. I was attending a great little conference called TODCon in Orlando. At the conference, I became friends with Adobe Evangelist Greg Rewis and his soon-to-be-wife Stephanie Sullivan, and they in turn introduced me to a then-new social networking application called Twitter. Over the weekend, I played around with Twitter a bit, but updating my status via my computer seemed a bit clunky. Partially, that was due to the fact that Twitter's website is not all that great (something that it has still not fixed), but mostly due to the fact that the nature of the site lent itself to being able to update your status anywhere, any time. I saw Greg and Stef doing that on their phones, and for the first time, I wanted a phone that was capable of more.

Thus, it was really Twitter that led me to purchase my first smartphone. At that time I was a T-Mobile customer; however, the obvious choice back in the summer of 2009 was the G1, the first Android-based smartphone.

WHICH VERSION OF ANDROID DO I HAVE?

Android is an operating system like Windows or Mac OS. Well, honestly, it's a bit more like iOS, which runs the iPhone, iPod touch, and iPad, since like iOS, Android has been specifically designed to run on mobile devices. Today, many dozens of devices run on Android, from phones to tablets to televisions.

Like all software, Android has undergone a series of revisions, with Google pushing out new versions of the software on a regular basis. Also like all software, each version is referred to by both a formal version number and a less formal code name or nickname. To date, all of the nicknames for Android have been pastries and other tasty snacks. (Google must not feed its developers well.)

The first publicly released version of Android, version 1.1, was made available on February 9, 2009. First-generation Android-based phones, such as the G1 for T-Mobile, initially were based on version 1.1.

In April 2009, Google released Android 1.5, otherwise known as Cupcake. It was followed in September 2009 by Donut, or version 1.6. Both of these updates introduced exciting new features, such as a video camera and improved market experience.

A little over a month after the release of Donut came Éclair, Android 2.0 (which very quickly was followed by 2.0.1). Also, code-named Éclair, version 2.1 followed shortly thereafter in January 2010. Éclair added a ton of new features, all of which required significant improvements in the hardware on the phones running it, which is the polite way of saying that Éclair represented the point at which Google left early adopters, like myself, behind, as first-generation phones like my G1 would not be able to support 2.0 or future updates.

Mid-2010 saw the release of Android 2.2, nicknamed FroYo. For those of us who aren't as obsessed with sweets as the folks at Google, FroYo is the trade name for frozen yogurt. FroYo increased the speed and memory capabilities of Android and adds some exciting new features such as the ability to store applications on your device's memory card, and USB tethering, which allows you to use your phone's 3G data connection as a wireless hotspot for your computer's laptop. The market saw a rush in new applications built specifically for FroYo, including Adobe's Flash Player, which enables those with this version of the OS to surf the actual web.

Version 2.3, or Gingerbread, was released in December 2010. Gingerbread represented a fairly significant shift in the user interface and wider hardware support. As of this writing, FroYo and Gingerbread represent the version of Android on the widest variety of mobile phones.

In early 2011, Motorola released the Xoom, an Android tablet running Honeycomb, or Android version 3.0. Honeycomb has a radically different user interface from prior versions, designed specifically with tablets in mind. In fact, Honeycomb has never been released for phones. Almost all tablets that have shipped through 2011 run Honeycomb.

Late 2011 will see the release of Ice Cream Sandwich, which will see Android reunite its phone and tablet operating systems under a single version.

In addition to these official versions, several so-called "flavors" of Android are available, offered by the various device manufacturers. Currently, four such flavors of Android exist. Vanilla or "stock" Android is the version officially offered by Google. Devices with this flavor often receive major upgrades such as the latest version of the operating system before those with the other flavors. HTC, one of the leading manufacturers of Android devices, has a flavor known as Sense that adds a lot of custom home screen widgets. The other leading device manufacturer, Motorola, installs a custom version on many of its phones. Finally, Samsung offers TouchWiz as its customized flavor of Android on many of its devices.

SETTING UP YOUR ANDROID DEVICE

When you first purchase a new phone, the salesperson likely will take you through the process of setting up your phone. Most of the steps are things that she needs to do, such as creating your account with the wireless provider. The final few steps, however, will be done by you. The most important of

> **NOTE**
>
> The significant change that has occurred in the Android, and in fact the mobile, world since the printing of the first edition of this book is the introduction of tablets. Tablets inhabit a world somewhere between your phone and your laptop: They are obviously bigger and, in most cases at least, more powerful than your phone, but not nearly as powerful or functional as your laptop.
>
> I am being very careful and intentional about my use of terminology in this edition. Where something applies to only a phone or only a tablet, I will use the appropriate term. However, when what I am describing applies equally to either, I will use the more generic device.

these is either setting up a Google account or logging into your existing e-mail and social networking accounts.

GETTING A GOOGLE ACCOUNT

You need an account with Google in order to use most of the services available on Android. (Don't worry, you can still use a different kind of e-mail if you want.) The account is free and takes only a few moments to set up. If you already have a Google account, you can skip this section and move on to the fun stuff that follows.

You will be able to set up a Google account directly on your phone when you get it, but you can also do it in advance on your computer. Go to Google's home page, and click Sign in in the top-right corner. On the next page, click create an account for free. The sign-up form is fairly straightforward; unless you've been living on Mars for the last decade or so, I'm sure you've filled out a dozen or so forms like this before. You need to give them a current e-mail address and create a password. They have a cool little widget that tells you how strong your password is; because this password will be the gatekeeper for all of your Google information, including a lot of data you will get from your phone, you want to make it as strong as possible.

WHAT MAKES A GOOD PASSWORD?

A good, strong password protects your data in the same way a good, strong deadbolt protects your house. The first rule in making a good password is to pick something that has nothing at all to do with you personally. A very common method of trying to get someone's password is a method known as "social engineering." Many people pick passwords that relate to their personal life in some way — a child's or spouse's name, the name of a pet, an anniversary date or birthday, or something similar. Keep in mind that in these days of hyper-connectivity, a person doesn't need to know you to get this data, as it can be gleaned from Facebook, other social networking sites, or even by simply doing a search on your name. If the obvious passwords don't work, the next thing the hacker will try to do is known as a brute-force attack. I'm sure you've seen movies in which the barbarian hordes try to beat down the castle gates with a battering ram, the theory being that even the strongest gates eventually will crack if you hit them repeatedly enough times. Brute-force password attacks work on the same theory,

only with fewer sweaty, foul-smelling soldiers and less blood. Instead of a battering ram, the hacker uses a computer program that simply keeps entering passwords until it stumbles across the right one. Although a truly determined hacker might try every possible combination of letters, most will instead rely on dictionaries, starting with "a" and going through "zythum," or something along those lines. Conventional wisdom at this point suggests that using a combination of random upper- and lowercase letters, numbers and special characters is the way to go, so your password should look something like what they use to replace swear words in comic strips. The problem with that approach, however, is that such a password becomes increasingly more difficult to remember, and is likely going to be at best frustrating to attempt to input on a virtual keyboard on your mobile device. So instead of something like $3r3Ni7y, try a sentence of uncommon words, like "buffy is spiffy". While a lot of systems that require so-called strong passwords will balk at that, a recent look at the usability of passwords, available online at www.baekdal.com/tips/password-security-usability, shows that such a password would take almost 40 million years to crack using a dictionary attack.

The next set of options on the form isn't terribly relevant to setting up your device. Personally, I do use Google as my desktop browser's home page, but nothing bad will happen if you choose not to. Your location and birthday are in there, as far as I can figure, so that Google can collect demographic data on its customers. I've had a Google account for many years, and I've never so much as received a card on my birthday. The word verification is needed to make it more difficult for spammers to create accounts. You can read the "Terms of Service" (TOS) if you want, but I suspect that it is just a bunch of legal mumbo-jumbo; I know I've never read a TOS in my life. Click "I accept. Create my account," and you're done.

SYNCHING YOUR DEVICE WITH YOUR ACCOUNT

After you have your phone unpackaged and charged and you've created your Google account, you can synchronize the two. This will give your device access to the same data as you have on your computer; for example, if you choose to use Gmail, Google's e-mail service, you will be able to use it from either your device or your computer. This synchronization is very easy: Simply enter your Google username, which will be the e-mail address you used when you registered for the account, and your password into your device and then give the service a minute or so to do its magic. Note that some people who have had accounts with Google for a long time might have a distinct username, rather than an e-mail address.

ACCESSORIES

With Android sales rising rapidly, more and more accessories are becoming available all the time. Following is a list of some of the most essential accessories to consider purchasing. You can find many of these accessories at the same store where you purchased your phone or online at sites such as www.androidcentral.com.

◇ Car charger (see Figure 1.1). You are likely going to want to invest in a car charger to keep the phone charged while you drive. This is particularly important if you're going to use Navigation, the turn-by-turn GPS directions application (see Chapter 7 for details on Navigation). Navigation is one of the truly awesome applications available, particularly since it is free, but it will drain your battery very quickly, so I always make sure to keep my phone plugged in when I use Navigation. Most Android devices charge via a USB port, so car chargers may be interchangeable between them. Unfortunately, almost all current devices

Figure 1.1

A car charger with the micro USB connector

have moved from a mini USB port to a smaller and appropriately named micro USB port, so my G1 charger would not work with my Droid X, but the Droid X charger works fine with my wife's LG Ally Android phone. In the interest of completeness, I should mention that most tablets unfortunately use a custom charger, so if you want to keep your tablet powered on the road, you will need a special car charger for it.

◇ Screen protectors (see Figure 1.2). Your screen really is your device, and

Figure 1.2

A set of screen protectors; be sure to buy a brand designed specifically for your model of device.

if it becomes too scratched or damaged, you will not be able to use your device at all. Thus, invest immediately in some screen protectors. These clear plastic sheets stick to your screen and absorb all of the scratches and a lot of the other abuse your phone is likely to endure. When one becomes too scratched, simply peel it off and apply another. Just be sure to carefully clean the screen before applying the protector, or else you will end up with unsightly bubbles.

◇ Headphones or Bluetooth device (see Figure 1.3). As of this writing, 69 countries have laws applying to all or part of the nation (13 states and 12 additional municipalities in the United States) making it illegal to talk on your phone while driving unless you use a hands-free device of some kind. Therefore, this accessory can be seen more as a legal requirement. Keep in mind, though, that you will not only be talking on your phone, as your Android device also will be your MP3 player, podcast player, in-car navigation system, and much more. All of these require

Figure 1.3

A standard set of headphones that I use to listen to my phone that you be able to hear the device, which in turn requires a headset or Bluetooth device. Pretty much every device includes a standard headphone jack, so any headphones you already own for your MP3 player or other devices will work, at least for listening to music and movies. However, you will need some other device— likely a Bluetooth headset—in order to talk into your phone without holding it. If using a Bluetooth headset is not your thing (I find them to be extremely uncomfortable), you can also look into a Bluetooth speaker, such as the Motorola Roadster (see Figure 1.4).

◇ Car mount (see Figure 1.5). This allows you to mount your phone on your dashboard, which can be very helpful when using Navigation and when using the phone as an alternative to your car stereo. When you insert your phone into the car mount, it switches to a special car mode. For more details on Car mode and using the car mount, see Chapter 7. Your car mount may include a car charger.

Figure 1.4

A Bluetooth headset

◇ Extra storage (see Figure 1.6). Most devices today include the ability to add storage with a MicroSD memory card. As the name implies, these cards are similar to the larger SD card you already may be using for your digital camera, only smaller. Your device will almost certainly have a MicroSD card in it when you purchase, but you should check to see whether you can replace it with one with a larger capacity.

◇ Protective case (see Figure 1.7). A protective case may reduce damage if the device is dropped. I have a soft gel that wraps around the back of the phone and has the advantage of being very easy to remove, which is handy since I cannot place the phone in the car mount with the case on. For my tablet, I invested in a Belkin folio that not only protects the tablet, but also allows me to prop it up for easier use.

◇ Micro USB cable (see Figure 1.8). One of these cables should have come with your device, but as you will need this cable to charge your phone as well as connect it to your computer to transfer files, you may want one or two extras. I keep one plugged into the wall charger, another plugged into the computer, and a third in the bag with my laptop, thus ensuring that I will be able to plug my phone in just about anywhere. If you have a tablet, you will not be able to use the micro USB to charge it, even off your computer. You will still need the cable to connect your tablet to your computer to transfer files.

Figure 1.5

A car mount for the Droid X

Figure 1.6

The 16GB MicroSD card, on the left, came preinstalled in my Droid X. The 8GB SD card on the right is shown for scale.

Figure 1.7

A soft gel case, one of many styles available

Figure 1.8

A micro USB cable

THE HOME SCREEN

The home screen in Android is like the desktop on your computer (see Figure 1.9). It provides a place for you to place shortcuts to your favorite and most-used applications. You can also customize your home screen with widgets for applications that display the time, up-to-the-minute stock quotes or sports scores, the song you currently are listening to, Google search, and much more. You can set the background to anything you like. See Chapter 3 for information on adding shortcuts and widgets to your home screen.

You can access the home screen any time on your phone by pressing the Home button. All Android phones include a button on the phone itself, usually with an icon representing a house, to go to the home screen. Figure 1.10 shows it on a Motorola Droid X. Tablets running Honeycomb feature a virtual Home button, found in the Actions bar at the bottom of the screen (see Figure 1.11).

The home screen actually is composed of several different screens. Depending on the version and flavor of Android on your device, you should have between three and seven screens. Each of these screens works the same as each of the others, providing

Figure 1.9

The main home screen on my Droid X

a place to put shortcuts and widgets. You can move between screens by sliding your finger to the right or left. Some devices also provide small icons you can use to quickly access your other screens.

See Chapter 3 for more details on customizing and working with your home screen.

THE APPLICATIONS LAUNCHER

You are likely to have more applications than can fit on your home screen, so Android provides the Applications Launcher to store the rest of them. On

Figure 1.10

The Home button on the Droid X

most phones, the launcher can be accessed by tapping the button found at the bottom of the screen, while Honeycomb on tablets places it in the top-right corner of the screen. The launcher automatically lists all of your installed applications alphabetically. You can scroll through them by simply sliding your finger up on the screen. Touch an application to launch it.

ORGANIZING YOUR APPLICATIONS

In newer versions of Android, including Gingerbread, you can organize your applications into groups to help keep you from having to scroll through many dozens of applications to find the one you want. When you access the Applications Launcher, select the All apps icon at the top of the screen, then select New group. Enter a name that will describe the applications you are placing in the group, then select the disk icon to save the group (see Figure 1.12). Finally, select the green arrow in the top-right corner, and choose the apps you want in the group.

Once you have created the group, you can access it by returning to the Applications Launcher, selecting All apps, and then selecting the group.

Figure 1.11

The Home button on Honeycomb Action bar

Figure 1.12
Creating a new group

THE NOTIFICATIONS BAR

The top of your phone's screen is the Notifications Bar, an area where the operating system and applications give you alerts to let you know what is going on. The right side of the bar is reserved for the operating system to display things like the time, battery charge, and data connectivity. The left side is an area for running applications or where the operating system displays notifications. Table 1.1 shows some of the more common icons you will find on the bar. Note that you will not always see these

Table 1.1
Common Android Notification Icons

Icon	What it Means
	An alarm is on.
	Bluetooth is active on your phone.
	Bluetooth device is connected.
	GPS is active.
	Wi-Fi is active.
	An application is currently downloading.
	The phone is set to vibrate.
	Sounds are turned off.
	The indicator for network strength
3G	You are connected to a 3G network.
	Your phone is in Airplane mode.
	Your phone is synching with Google's servers.
	You are connected via USB to a computer.
	Battery is full.
	Battery is partially full.
	Battery is charging.
	An application has finished downloading and installing.
	You are currently making a call.
	You have voice mail.
	You have an unread text message.
	Phone is connected to a car mount.
	Connection for Media Share is detected.
	Application updates are available.

icons, and some of them will occasionally appear while a process is running, so unless you happen to glance at your screen at the right moment, you may not see it at all. Also, you may install additional applications that add their own notification icons.

If you need to see details on your notifications, you can pull the Notifications Bar down. Simply press your finger anywhere on the bar and drag down to expand it to fit your screen. Depending on the applications you have running, you should see details of the notifications, such as the number of applications that need updating or the number of unread e-mail messages you have.

In Gingerbread, you can dismiss each notification separately, or dismiss them all.

THE ACTION BAR

If you have a tablet running Honeycomb, you will have an Action bar at the bottom of the screen, rather than a Notifications Bar at the top. While the two have a lot in common, the Action bar is a major improvement over the older Notifications Bar.

The left side of the Action bar includes buttons that make up for the lack of physical buttons on tablets. The first of these buttons is a Back button. Depending on the application, selecting it will either take you back to a prior screen or state in an application, or it may return you to another application, or possibly the home screen. Next to the Back button is the Home button, which displays your home screen. The third button is new to Honeycomb, and not duplicated on phones. Selecting this button—it looks like two rectangles stacked on top of each other—displays all currently running applications and allows you to quickly jump from one to another.

Android phones include a physical Menu button, although not all applications make use of it. On a Honeycomb tablet, if you are running an application that uses the Menu, a fourth button will often appear to the right of the multitask button that allows you to access the menu.

The right side of the Action bar more closely resembles the Notifications Bar on older Android devices. Here you will find notifications from applications such as new mail or Tweets, currently playing music, and the like. You will also find the clock, network notification, and battery life indicators. An important difference in Honeycomb is that each of these notifications can be selected independently, and application developers can choose to add additional information to them. For example, if you select the icon informing you that you have new mail, a pop-up will appear showing you the important details of the message, including the sender and subject. Selecting the icon for currently playing music brings up a display that not only lets you know the current song and artist, but also allows you to pause, jump to the prior song, and jump to the next song (see Figure 1.13).

The far-right section of the Notifications Bar in older versions was not selectable, but in Honeycomb, you can tap on the clock, network notification, and battery indicator to display a larger pop-up showing the network to which you are connected and the exact amount of remaining battery charge. You can also access the rest of your notifications from here.

DEVICE SETTINGS

This is an area where you can customize much of the device's functionality, which

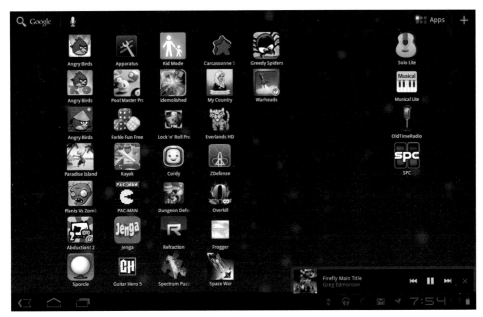

Figure 1.13

The notification for Google Music on Honeycomb, providing basic playback controls from the Actions bar

is very similar to the way you can use the Windows Control Panel to customize your PC.

On most phones, you can access the settings by pressing your phone's Menu button while on the home screen (see Figure 1.14). When you dig into specific settings, you can use your phone's Back button to return to the previous screen. On a tablet with Honeycomb, you can access the settings by tapping the time, network notification or battery indicator on the Actions bar, then selecting the network icon in the pop-up, and finally selecting Settings. Settings is also available in the Applications Launcher in any version.

The precise options available in the settings will vary slightly from one phone to the next and even from one carrier to

the next, but in general, they contain the same basic groups of settings, as shown in Table 1.2.

Other devices may include additional settings. For example, the Droid X also includes an HDMI settings screen for connecting your device to a high-definition television or projector. See Chapter 9 for more details on this feature. Verizon includes a feature on its service plans called Backup Assistant to help back up your phone's data, so Verizon's phones also include a settings widget for it.

WIRELESS AND NETWORK SETTINGS

Your device has a wide variety of controls to deal with wireless connectivity. You can access these controls from your phone's Set-

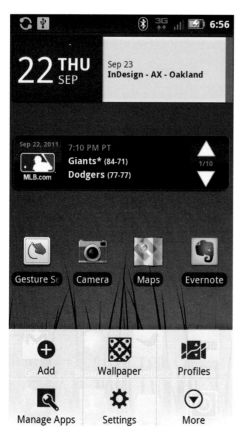

Getting to Settings from the home screen

Although the actual science behind whether a device could interfere with a plane and bring it down is still a matter of debate, the law is clear. Generally, your device needs to be completely powered off during takeoff and until the plane reaches 10,000 feet and then again once the plane descends below 10,000 feet until it lands. Between those times, however, you can use your device to listen to music, play games, read books, watch movies—any of the activities you can do without data connections. By the way, if a flight attendant tells you to turn off your phone even above 10,000 feet and even when it is in Airplane mode, I would suggest that you do so. It really is not worth having to spend your time talking to the authorities when you land.

The next setting available is a simple toggle that enables you to turn Wi-Fi on or off. When I purchased my first Android phone, the Google G1, I asked the T-Mobile salesman what the heck 3G was, since it seemed to be one of those terms that people like to throw around but actually have no idea what it really is. I don't honestly think he did, either, but he gave me a plausible answer nonetheless: 3G provides, in his words, "high-speed-like connections to the phone." What does "high-speed-like" mean, exactly? Well, in short, it means that you are not getting actual high-speed Internet access, but if you are old enough to remember surfing the web on 56K modems, it is not quite that slow. In practice, it turns out to be somewhere in between most of the time. However, your device does not have to use 3G at all if you do not want it to. Instead, if you are within range of a Wi-Fi connection, you can switch over to that and get true high-speed. If you want the convenience of a tablet with-

tings application. See the previous section for details on getting to the settings, but when there, select the first option: Wireless & Networks.

The first option in this screen turns Airplane mode on or off, which disables all connections into and out of your device (see Figure 1.15). As its name implies, it is designed for when you are in an airplane. Airplane mode is important because in the United States, it is illegal to have your device turned on and potentially transmitting data while the plane you are in is in flight.

Table 1.2

Settings Categories

Category	General Uses
Wireless & Networks	Allows access to turn Wi-Fi on and off and configure settings to allow the phone to connect to (or serve as) Wi-Fi hotspots, as well as Bluetooth settings and other mobile networks.
Call Settings	From here, you can set up your voice mail, configure call forwarding and call waiting, and other options relating to using your phone as a phone. See Chapter 4 for details on using your phone as, well, a phone. Obviously, this is not available on tablets.
Sound	Set ringtones, notification sounds, and volume.
Display	You can also configure the screen's brightness and how long the screen will stay on.
Battery & Data Manager	Use these controls to configure which applications can remain synchronized with online services. Data manager is not available on tablets; battery manager may not be listed as a separate setting and will instead be available in the About section.
Location & Security	Set your location and manage security settings such as requiring pattern input to unlock your phone.
Accounts	Manage your Google, social networking, and carrier-specific accounts.
Applications	Control running applications and uninstall applications you no longer want.
Search	Customize Google search settings.
Applications	See a complete list of applications and how much space they are taking. You can also uninstall applications from here, or force them to close if they stop working.
Privacy	Configure settings to back up and restore data and perform a factory reset of the device
Storage	Mounts or unmounts the SD card to allow access to it from a desktop computer and enables you to see how much space you have left.
Date & Time	Set the formats for date and time display.
Language & Keyboard	Controls the language and regional settings of the phone.
Accessibility	Enables options to make your phone easier to use if you have a disability such as reduced hearing or vision, or a mobility impairment: Only available on phones.
About phone or tablet	Find out which version of Android you are using, what applications are chewing up your battery, and, if you really want to, read a bunch of legalese about Android.

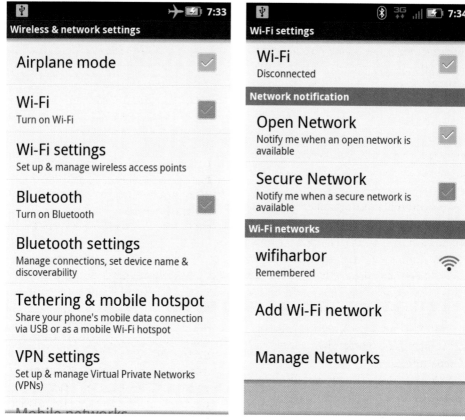

Figure 1.15
The phone with Airplane mode enabled; notice that the signal indicator now displays an airplane.

Figure 1.16
Available Wi-Fi networks

out paying for a contract with a wireless provider, you can purchase a Wi-Fi-only device. Using Wi-Fi, you can still surf the Internet, play games, listen to music, and download new applications.

To connect to a Wi-Fi network, you need to turn Wi-Fi on, and you also need to tell your device that you want to connect to a network by selecting Wi-Fi. These settings display all of the networks in range of your device and their relative signal strength (see Figure 1.16). If I select a secure net-

work to which I am not connected, I will be prompted to enter the key code for that network. Assuming I enter the correct code, my device will connect to that network and then remember it, automatically connecting any time it comes in range. When I select a network to which I am connected, I can see status information for that network. Remembered networks also will display on the main list of networks, even if they are not in range. If you want to remove a network you no longer want to use, press and hold on a network and you'll get an option to "forget" it.

Press your device's Back button to return to the Wireless & Network Settings screen, where you can enable Bluetooth and configure the settings using the next two controls on the main Wireless Settings screen. In order to use a Bluetooth headset, you need to enter its name, although if you select the Scan for Devices control, your device automatically will discover the headset. See Chapter 4 for more details on setting up and using Bluetooth.

Many corporate networks allow employees to access protected internal network documents using a Virtual Private Network, VPN. Assuming you have proper access to a VPN, you can use the VPN settings screen, accessible from the main Wireless & Network Settings screen, to configure your connection. If you do not know how to connect to your VPN, contact your company's IT department.

The Mobile Networks settings allow you to control what happens when you leave your carrier provider's coverage area. Be aware that many providers charge handsomely for the privilege of using your phone outside their coverage area. In 2009, I had the opportunity to teach a class on Grand Cayman Island and discovered that my carrier at the time was going to charge me more than $1 per minute just to have my phone on and connected to some foreign network. That cost did not include the cost of making any calls. Data charges were even worse, at $1.50 per megabyte. The web is full of horror stories of people travelling abroad and returning home to cell phone bills in the thousands of dollars. You can avoid these charges by setting your phone to the Home only option in the settings. When I travel overseas, I keep my

TIDBIT

Just a year after writing the first edition of this book, 3G is already old-school. Now, all the rage for people marketing mobile devices is "4G." If you watch TV at all, you likely have seen the commercials for the major carriers in which they each try to claim that they have more or better or faster 4G coverage. However, some inquiring minds might wonder whether there was ever a 1G or 2G, before we got the 3G and 4G. The answer, in short, is yes. 3G is defined, rather dryly, by Wikipedia as "International Mobile Telecommunications-2000 (IMT — 2000), better known as 3G or 3rd Generation, is a generation of standards for mobile phones and mobile telecommunications services fulfilling specifications by the International Telecommunication Union." 3G actually stands for "3rd Generation," which, of course, means that there must have been a 1st and 2nd generation. 1G was in fact the mobile technology used by the first mobile phones in the 1980s. It is worth noting, however, that the 1G moniker was applied only to these phones in retrospect, after 2G was adopted in the early 1990s. Neither was really exciting enough to be worth advertising, which is why 3G was the first one that anyone ever heard about.

LTE is an acronym for the even-more-nonsensical "Long Term Evolution." In its current implementation, LTE provides speeds somewhere between 3G and 4G, although you would never know that it is anything other than 4G from the commercials. A newer technology, LTE Advanced, seeks to bring it in line with 4G.

phone in Airplane mode, just to be on the safe side.

RINGTONES

Ringtones can be a highly personal and, of course, highly annoying, feature of your phone. Android phones allow you to set a default ringtone from one of about a few dozen choices out of the box. Later, when you have music uploaded to your phone, you can use those songs as your ringtone, which is discussed in Chapter 8. You also can set specific ringtones for specific people, which is covered in Chapter 4. For now, we want to look at setting a default ringtone.

In the main Settings screen, select Sound & Display. Then select Phone ringtone. A list of the default ringtones will display. Touch each in turn to listen to it. When you find one you like, tap OK. Back on the Sound & Display Settings screen, you can set the volume of the ringtone using Ringer volume; simply slide your finger along the slider to increase or decrease the volume.

Another important default sound is the Notification ringtone, which is the sound that plays whenever your phone or an application wants to let you know that something is happening. Like the call ringtone, you can select from a list of default notification sounds, or you can further customize it using third-party applications.

SILENCING YOUR RINGTONE

Although I am sure that you have never forgotten to turn off your ringer when sitting in an important meeting, you, of course, know people who have. On Android, you have a few methods by which you can silence your phone. The easiest method,

only available on most (but not all) newer devices, is to use the slider on the phone's lock screen (see Figure 1.17). The easiest way to get to the lock screen is to press the power button once to dim the phone, then again to wake it. (Don't worry, you're not actually turning it off.)

If your phone is not already asleep, you can go into the Sound & Display settings and tap the first option: Silent mode. A quicker method, though, is available anywhere on your phone: Press and hold the power button for 2–3 seconds. On the

Figure 1.17

Silencing the phone from the Lock screen

Droid X, this button is located on top of the phone. Other older models may use the End Call button (if there is one). You will see a menu appear that enables you to silence your phone or, if it is already silenced, turn the sound back on. This menu also allows you to quickly enter and exit Airplane mode.

Phones that are running Android 2.1 or below can be silenced by pressing the volume-down button repeatedly, which will cycle through the different volume levels (my Droid X has 15 of them), through vibrate mode, and finally to silent mode. This function was removed in Android 2.2.

Some phones such as the Droid X include a great feature known as the Smart Sensor to help keep you from embarrassing yourself by leaving the ringer on when you do not mean to. These settings are located at the very bottom of the Sound & Display settings. Unfortunately, neither of these settings is clearly explained on the phone. The first, Double-Tap to Silence, enables you to quickly silence the ringtone when a call comes in by double-tapping. It does not completely free you from the glares of your boss and co-workers, because the phone will likely begin ringing before you realize a call is coming in, but it will be the fastest way to shut the thing up. The second, Smart Profile: Face Down to Vibrate, lets you simply flip the phone over on its face to put it in vibration mode when an alert or call comes in.

ORIENTATION AND THE ACCELEROMETER

The accelerometer is one of the coolest features of modern devices. Essentially, it is the function of that device that knows which direction the device is moving. Some

ALTERNATE APP

The worst part about turning your ringer off is remembering to turn it back on. As a teacher, I need to turn my ringer off almost every day. For a long time, I was plagued with the problem of forgetting to turn it back on when my class was over, causing me to miss important calls in the evening. I ran into a similar problem while traveling: I like to use my phone as an alarm clock in hotels, but that meant leaving the ringer on and being disturbed in the night by e-mail notifications and the like (including the occasional odd call). Both of these problems were solved when I discovered Shush! Ringer Restorer. This great app launches whenever you silence your phone—whether by turning the ring volume all the way down or using the lock screen—and asks you how long you would like your ringer off. You simply drag a slider around a circle to set the desired time, and the app will turn your ringer back on for you. It's great for meetings, movies, hotels, and anywhere else you need to silence your phone for a set amount of time. Best of all, it's free. Search for it in the Android Market and download it today. I promise you won't regret it.

pretty cool games rely on the accelerometer, but so does a basic function of the device. Although the normal way most people hold a phone lends itself to a portrait orientation, in which the screen is taller than it is wide (the opposite seems to hold true with tablets, which tend to be held in a landscape orientation most of the time), the accelerometer can let the device reorient itself when you turn it in your hand, so that even if you hold it sideways, everything will still be right-side up. Although this has an obvious use when watching a wide-screen movie or video, it can often be helpful when simply reading a web page or e-mail. You can do so in the Screen & Display settings. Why might you want to? The first edition of the book included a line where I said I could not think of a good reason to do it, but that was before I started reading books on the device. While I would still never turn off the accelerometer on my phone, I turn it off at times on the tablet to keep the orientation from rotating when I am reading an eBook. In fact, it happens frequently enough now that I wish there was a quicker way to disable it than going all the way into settings.

LOCK YOUR DEVICE

When you do not use your device for more than a few minutes, it will save battery life by turning off the screen. Different devices have different ways of waking it back up, mostly involving pressing one of the buttons, generally Home or the power button, on the device. When you wake up the device, you will need to unlock it by sliding the Unlock button (see Figure 1.18). Note that this does not necessary apply to tablets, which will generally go straight to the home screen upon waking.

You always have to consider the possibility of losing your phone, or even just setting out somewhere where others could get into it, say on your desk at work. Newer versions of Android have introduced several new ways to security lock your device. If you would like to prevent unauthorized use, you can lock the screen so that whenever you

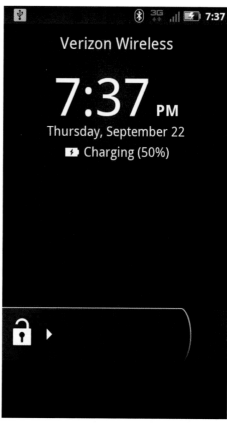

Figure 1.18
Unlocking the device

turn it back on or wake it up, you need to enter a special pattern. You configure this feature by going into the Location & Security settings and then scrolling down and selecting Screen lock.

Securing with a Pattern

From the Security settings, if necessary select Security lock type and then Pattern lock. If you use the pattern, you are presented with a screen that provides instructions. When you tap Next, you see an example of what you need to do, which involves drawing something that connects at least four of the dots. When you tap Next again, you can draw your own pattern. Tap Continue, and you will have to draw your pattern again to make sure you know what it is. When you tap Confirm, you will be taken back to the Settings screen. From here, you can set the Security lock timer, so you can control whether you need to enter the pattern every time the monitor is off or only when the phone has been idle, with the screen off, for a set period of time.

The next time your device's screen locks, you will need to provide the pattern again to unlock it. Should you decide at some point to remove this feature, return to the settings screen and deselect the Security lock pattern option. Note that you will have to provide your pattern again in order to turn this feature off.

Securing with a Passcode

Devices with Android 2.2 or later—including Honeycomb tablets—enable you to use a password instead of a pattern to lock. You access the password settings using the same process as outlined previously for the pattern, but selecting Security & Location, Security Lock, Security Lock Type, and finally Passcode Lock. You are presented with a numeric grid that you can use to enter your passcode, which must be at least four digits. Type in the code you want to use and select the check mark in the lower-left corner. You need to enter the code a second time to confirm it. Then the next time your device locks, you need to enter the passcode to unlock it.

STORAGE

You can use the MicroSD card as additional storage for the data on your phone. By default, any pictures or videos you take with

> ### TIP
>
> Your device gives you five attempts at the pattern. After that, it locks itself down for 30 seconds. When this timeout is finished, you will see a "Forgot pattern?" button. Selecting this brings up a screen that allows you to unlock your device by entering your Google username and password. When entered correctly, your device will unlock and take you right to the pattern screen where you can create a new pattern that you will, at least hopefully, remember this time.

the device's camera will be stored on the card, as will application data such as your contacts and high scores on your games. If your device is running at least Android 2.2, you can even store some applications on the card.

Every device has a slightly different place to insert the MicroSD card, so you need to read the manual that came with your phone to find it (see Figure 1.19). If you are the type who likes to throw the manual away, unread, the very second you open the box, then you can find instructions online. Be aware that every device has a limit as to how big of a card it can read, so be sure to check that before you waste money on a card that is too big for your device.

After you have the card in your device, you can transfer files to and from your computer. You simply need to plug the USB cable that came with your device or any micro USB cable into a standard USB jack on your computer. You should see an icon

Figure 1.19

The Droid X MicroSD card is accessed by removing the back cover, then the battery.

appear on the Notifications Bar telling you that the USB is connected. If you have it enabled, you also will hear the notification sound. Then pull down the Notifications Bar from the top of the screen and select the USB Connection notification.

On FroYo and Gingerbread, you have four options as to how your device should connect to your computer (see Figure 1.20). Traditionally, you attach a smartphone to a computer and mount the SD card as a USB drive so that you can transfer files. This is a long-established technology and is widely supported across a wide range of devices, from desktop and laptop computers to modern car stereos and more. The downside to this system, though, is that while you have the card mounted on the computer, the

device itself cannot read it, so for example, you would be unable to listen to music or view pictures stored on the card via the device while you have it mounted. This is USB Mass Storage mode. However, a newer method, called PC mode, allows for two-way communication, so both your computer and your device retain full access to the card. The Windows Media Sync mode is intended to streamline synchronizing media files, such as music, between your computer and your device. Finally, Charge Only simply lets your phone know that it is plugged in to charge the battery and that you do not intend to transfer files. This mode can be helpful when you plug the device into a computer in a tightly restricted office environment that might disallow installing the

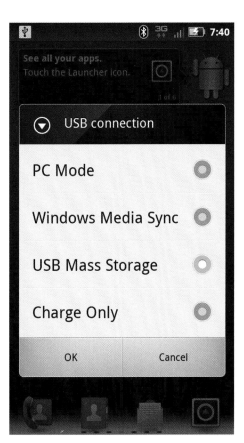

Figure 1.20
Choosing the mode to use to connect to the computer

TIP

You should avoid simply unplugging your device from the USB cord when it is connected to the computer and using the USB Storage option, as this might cause the files on the card to become corrupt. Instead, you should eject the USB drive from your computer and then remount the smart card on your device. The process of ejecting the drive differs depending on the operating system installed on your computer, but on most modern versions of Windows you can right-click the USB icon on your task tray and select Eject. On a Mac, you can generally simply drag the drive's icon to the trash can. On your device, you should go back to the same USB Settings menu you used to mount the drive originally and select unmount.

necessary drivers or transferring files to your device. Note that because tablets generally cannot be charged via USB, this final option will not be available.

At this point, if you are using Windows, you will get a dialog box on your machine asking how you want to deal with the new drive that suddenly appeared, since your computer may see your device as an additional hard drive. Some devices, when connected to a Windows 7 computer, display a special Control Panel window that provides information about the phone and

links to tasks such as synching media and transferring files. I generally select the Open folder to view files option to open Windows Explorer, at which point I can simply drag files from my computer's drive to the device or vice versa. The procedure is essentially the same if you are on a Mac.

TEXT INPUT

While some Android-based phones include a physical keyboard, and Bluetooth keyboards exist for tablets, all have an onscreen keyboard you can use. Typing on an onscreen keyboard can be a challenge, but after you get used to it, I think you'll find it fairly easy to use. My wife's Droid 2 has a physical keyboard, and yet most of the time when I use her phone, I rely on the onscreen keyboard at least as often as I do the physical one.

The Language & Keyboard Settings screen provides you with some options to control your keyboard. From the main Settings screen, tap Language & Keyboard, which will display the Text settings.

Multitouch Keyboard

An ever-expanding range of devices ship with two possible text input methods: the multitouch keyboard or Swype. The default multitouch keyboard functions as a simple on-screen keyboard that appears automatically whenever you are in a text field of any kind. You can select the arrow key in the lower-right corner for Shift, or the key below it to display numbers and special characters. Additional characters are available by tapping the Alt key.

The Text Settings screen does provide a few additional settings for the multitouch keyboard. You can turn on vibration and sound for key presses and enable auto-capitalization and auto-punctuation, both of which will save you a considerable number of taps when entering longer blocks of text. The keyboard also includes suggestions for words as you type and auto-correction.

If your phone has a physical keyboard, the on-screen keyboard will not likely appear if you have the physical keyboard out, so you need to be sure to keep the phone collapsed if you want to use the on-screen keyboard. The same applies if you have a Bluetooth keyboard joined to your tablet.

Swype

The other input method provided by default on some devices is Swype, an appli-

cation that greatly simplifies inputting text into your phone. If you have it, you can enable Swype by selecting it as the input method.

Swype takes some getting used to, and you will need to practice a bit to fully get the hang of things. After you have it figured out, I suspect you will love it. Swype allows you to trace paths across the keyboard to spell words, rather than having to tap each letter individually (see Figure 1.21). As you trace the path, the software guesses what letters

Figure 1.21

Tracing the word Google on the Swype keyboard

you wish to use and from that, guesses the word you are trying to spell. Saying that Swype is guessing might imply that it is not very accurate, but in fact, you will be surprised at how often it guesses correctly. When Swype is unsure, it prompts you with choices for words it thought you might be spelling.

DEVICE INFORMATION

The main Settings page also includes an About Phone page. From here, you can check to see whether you are eligible to upgrade to a new version of Android, to check your device's current status, and to find out the model number of your device and which version of Android you are running.

CHARGING

An unfortunate reality of all mobile devices is that they tend to like to use a lot of power. Although each generation of devices can remain unplugged longer, you should plan to keep your device plugged in as much as possible. You have three primary ways you can charge: a wall socket, car charger, and USB. Your device will have come with a wall charger, so simply plug it into any standard outlet and plug the other end into your device. The same applies to the car charger which like other devices, charges off of what used to be the cigarette lighter but is in most modern cars simply a power outlet. USB charging is perhaps the nicest method for phones, as you can charge your phone off of any computer with a USB plug. In fact, on many newer phones, the wall charger actually uses the same micro USB cable you rely on to connect and charge your phone off of your computer (see Figure 1.22). If you work

TIP

If your device did not come with Swype, you may still be able to get it by signing up for the company's beta program. It is free, and it provides copies of the software for devices that it is still testing on. Visit http://beta.swype.com/ for details.

in an environment with very tight computer restrictions whereby you cannot normally use USB devices, you need not worry; plugging the phone in to charge it does not necessarily mean you will be mounting the USB drive. You can, in fact, even charge your phone off a computer that is turned off, something I do frequently in hotels when I turn my laptop off to go to bed but keep my phone plugged into the computer and allow it to continue to charge. Charging off your computer is generally slower than charging off a wall outlet, so if you are in a hurry you should plug it into the wall. Tablets cannot charge off of USB, because the power requirements are greater. Therefore, to charge your tablet you will need to use either a wall charger or a car charger. The

Figure 1.22

A wall charger that uses a standard micro USB cable

TIDBIT

A new accessory that is becoming more popular is a portable or emergency charger. These small devices, which are usually about the size and weight of a smartphone and cost around $40, are basically portable battery packs. You charge them up, and then when you need a boost in power, you can plug your device in to recharge. How much charge you get from one of the devices depends on lots of factors, including the device doing the charging and the device needing to be charged, but if you think you may find yourself in a situation where you will be away from a power outlet for an extended period of time, such as over a long flight or during a conference, they provide a nice alternative to running out of power.

amount of time your device takes to charge will vary from one model to the next, but in general, you should allow several hours of charging if you have completely depleted the battery. Likewise, the amount of time you can go without charging will vary depending not only on the model of device you use but also on what applications you are running. Most devices should be able to go several days at least if you leave them alone, but may hold only a few hours' charge if you use battery-intensive applications such as anything involving GPS or Bluetooth.

Applications

The Skim

Early cell phones were just that—phones. Later, their capabilities began to expand to include texting, and eventually they allowed users to play simple games, take pictures, or browse web pages. Still, they were phones that could sort of act like computers. Today's smartphones, on the other hand, are portable computers first and foremost. They just happen to be computers that can, almost incidentally, make phone calls.

USING THE ANDROID MARKET

The Android Market is the primary resource to find applications for download. Although no requirement demands that developers use the Market, most will simply due to the visibility it provides their applications.

You can access the Market at any time using the application that comes preinstalled on your device (see Figure 2.1). The main screen on the Market application allows you to browse through popular featured applications, games, books, and movies.

The Apps tab brings up a new screen that displays categories of applications. Selecting one of these categories displays a list of

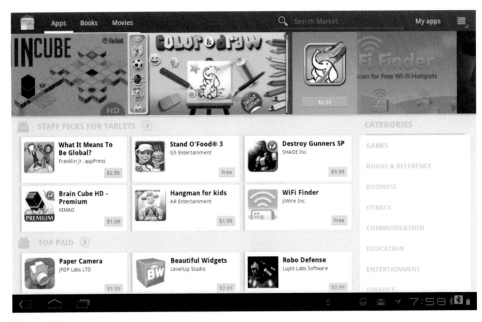

Figure 2.1

The Market main screen on Honeycomb

the applications in that category. You can view the list by a variety of criteria, depending on your version of Android. On Gingerbread, you can select Categories, Featured, Top Paid, Top Free, Top Grossing, Top New Paid, Top New Free, or Trending. Honeycomb adds Staff Picks

for Tablets to this list. Each application is listed by its name, the name of the developer, its cost, and its current user rating (see Figure 2.2).

Selecting an application brings up a page that shows the details of the application, screen shots, and user reviews (see Figure 2.3). At any point, you can use your device's Back button to return to either the application list or the main screen of the Market.

NOTE

Google updates the look and feel of the Market on a regular basis, so while the images in this section were accurate as of the time of this writing, they might not be by the time you read this.

SEARCHING FOR APPLICATIONS

If you have a particular application in mind, you can use the Market's search feature to find it. From the Market's main screen, select the search icon. Type the name or keywords of the application you want to find, then select the magnifying

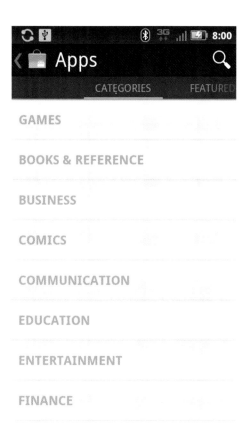

Figure 2.2
Application categories on Gingerbread

Figure 2.3
An application's information screen

glass icon to see a list of matching applications. As with browsing, the search list displays the name of the application, the name of the developer, the cost, and the rating of the application.

DOWNLOADING AND INSTALLING FREE APPLICATIONS

Many of the applications you will find in the Market are free. In fact, the Android Market has a higher percentage of free applications than any other mobile application marketplace, due in large part to the fact that Google imposes a much smaller initial fee for developers than some of its competitors do. When you find a free application that interests you, select the Install button at the bottom of the application's detail page. Your device then will display a message page detailing what services on the device the application will need access to (see Figure 2.4). Press OK, and the application will begin downloading.

You are returned to your most recent search or browse page, and the Notifications Bar will display an icon letting you know that the application is downloading. The Notifica-

Figure 2.4
The services needed by the application

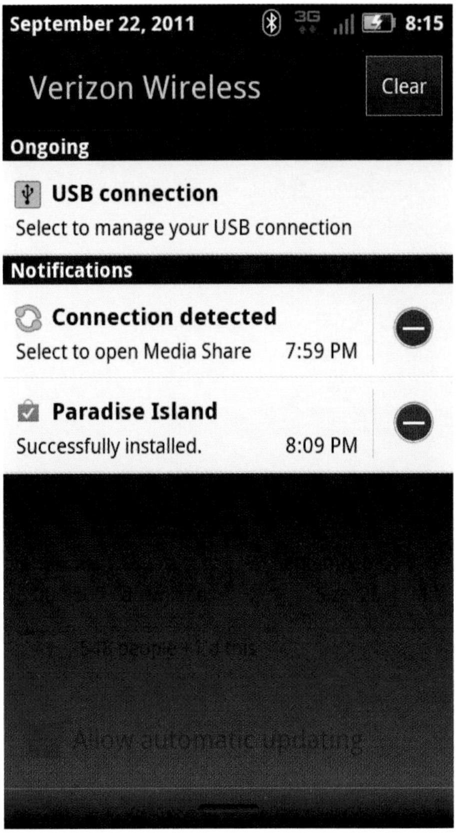

Figure 2.5
The application, ready to use

tion Bar will inform you after the download is complete, at which point you can select the application to launch it (see Figure 2.5).

PAYING FOR APPLICATIONS

If you decide to download an application that requires payment, you can purchase it directly through your device. Go to the page for the application and select Buy. As with free applications, the download process for paid apps begins with an information screen letting you know what services the application might use when it runs, plus an addi-

tional notification of the price and credit card attached to your account (see Figure 2.6). When you select Accept & buy, your application will download and install. You also will receive a confirmation e-mail for your purchase.

AMAZON APPSTORE FOR ANDROID

In March 2011, Amazon launched its own Android Appstore. The Appstore provides an alternate distribution channel for Android developers, leveraging the Amazon brand.

Figure 2.6
Purchasing the application

TIP

You can link a credit card to your Google account to simplify the process of purchasing applications. After it is linked, the card will display directly on the checkout screen, so you do not have to keep entering information over again. Entering these linked cards involves going to http://checkout.google.com, logging in with your Google account, and then entering the credit card information on the screen provided.

Once installed, you can use the Appstore much like you use the official Market. I, for one, have only used it to date to download the Free Apps of the Day, as the selection of other apps seems notably similar to those offered in the official Market.

One particularly nice feature of the Appstore is the Free App of the Day: Every day, an application that normally costs is offered for free (see Figure 2.7). The majority of the Free Apps of the Day to date have been games.

In order to access the Appstore, you need the Amazon Appstore app, which is not available in the Android Market. Instead, you need to visit www.amazon.com/appstore. From here, you will be able to enter an e-mail address that is accessible on your device. Amazon will e-mail that address with a link to the app.

TIP

You can get a full refund on any application purchased through the Android Market within 15 minutes of that purchase. To return an application and get a refund, go to the Downloads section of the market (usually by pressing the Menu button), select the application, and select Uninstall & Refund. If you only see an Uninstall button, then you are either looking at a free app or your 15-minute period has expired.

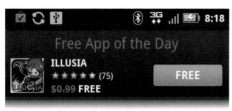

Save for Later **Share**

Product Description

Created by the makers of ZENONIA, ILLUSIA is a side-scrolling role playing game (RPG) containing all the core elements of traditional role playing with anime-style graphics. Explore the world through quests,

Customer Reviews ☆☆☆☆☆ (75)

Figure 2.7

One of the Free App of the Day offerings from the Amazon Appstore

TIDBIT

If you own an Amazon Kindle Fire, the company's tablet, you will only have access to the Amazon Appstore for apps, and not be able to use the standard Google Market.

DOWNLOADING AND INSTALLING APPLICATIONS FROM OTHER SOURCES

Android is a completely open system, so developers are not required to use the official Android Market to distribute their applications. Instead, developers are free to distribute their applications directly from their own websites or via alternate markets. In order to download an alternate application, you need to find its location online. You can download the APK file from the developer's site. If you are using your desktop or laptop computer, you need to transfer the application to your device via USB, by e-mail, or any other file-transfer method. You can then the install the application. You will also need to specifically enable this ability on your device by going into the device's Settings from your home screen, then tapping Applications and enabling the check box labeled Unknown sources. Unfortunately, some AT&T phones still restrict this functionality, so you will need to instead download the Sideload Wonder Machine app, available in the Google Market.

Many developers are providing an alternate and much easier way to install applications: QR codes, which look a lot like normal barcodes. You need to install the free Barcode Scanner app, available in the Android Market. Then when you encounter a barcode, you can scan the code using the device's camera. The application displays the location of the app it found, at which point you can select the link to download the app. Note that barcodes may be found on websites or in printed materials such as books and magazines, on buildings —anywhere, really. And they're not just for installing applications. They also can lead you to a web page, video, or any other online content.

KEEPING APPLICATIONS UP TO DATE

Android includes an automatic application update process by default. Whenever an application you have installed has an update, the Notifications Bar displays an icon letting you know that you have updates available. Expand the Notifications Bar, select Updates Available, which takes you to the My Downloads section of the Market. All apps that have current updates are displayed.

Select the app you want to update, and read through the information screen, which often has information on what exactly has been updated in the app. If you want to run the update, select Update, which prompts you to be sure that you want to replace the older version of the app with the new one. After you select OK, you are taken to the screen that notifies you which services the app will use, and then the application downloads and installs.

Beginning with Android 2.2, you have the option to set an application to update itself automatically, in the background, without needing your permission (other than the initial OK). However, if an application's permissions (the services that are listed when it's initially installed) are changing, you'll have to update the application manually as a security measure.

NOTE

In order to install the Appstore or apps you download from it, you will need to allow applications to be installed from other sources. See the following section for details on enabling this on your device. This does not apply to the Kindle Fire, which comes with Amazon Appstore preinstalled..

TIDBIT

Android 2.2 allows applications to be installed on your device's SD card, rather than on the device's internal memory. As the SD card provides expandable memory, this may allow you to install many more applications. Note, however, that this feature needs to be enabled by the application's developer, so it may not be possible on some, or even many, applications you download. Some widgets may not work if the application is installed on the card, and you may not be able to install if the card is mounted on your computer.

Your Home Screens

The Skim

When I teach introductory Windows classes, one of the first things students always want to learn is how to customize their desktop. I have, in fact, always been amazed by the number of students who take two or three classes on something else entirely and yet customize the desktop on the training center's computers. Your Android device offers almost as much customization as your computer. As with your computer, you can change most of the appearance of the device to make it more of an extension of your personality.

ADDING APPLICATION SHORTCUTS TO YOUR HOME SCREENS PRE-HONEYCOMB

Note that the following section applies to devices running Gingerbread or earlier. If you have a tablet running Honeycomb, please skip to the next section.

Once installed, all applications reside in the Applications Launcher. Although you can search through the launcher when you need an app, it will be easier if you add a shortcut to your home screen instead. You can add shortcuts by first opening the Applications Launcher and finding the app you want. Then long-press the app until you feel the phone vibrate and the Application Launcher collapses. Drop the app wherever you want on the home screen. You can also add shortcuts by long-pressing on your home screen and selecting Shortcuts. If you have an HTC Sense phone, you will find a plus icon on your home screen that you can tap to add shortcuts.

On many Gingerbread devices, Google made the process a bit more difficult. When you long-press the app in the Launcher, an additional screen appears with a set of options including Add to Home. Select this, then drag the app to the desired spot on the home screen. The problem here is that selecting the option to Add to Home requires that you lift your finger off the phone, so whereas the process used to be long-press and drag, it is now long-press, release, tap, then long-press and drag. I am not sure why the developers thought that this was an improvement, but I manage to miss long-pressing on the app in the final step at least half the time, requiring that I start the whole process over. Also, under the old system, you could drag an app out to a home screen that was full, and simply drag to the left or right edge of the screen to move to a new screen. In Gingerbread, if you start the process while on a full home screen, you will get an error after selecting Add to Home. Clearly, the usability testing folks at Google had the day off when this was implemented. Thankfully, some other implementations of Android, such as the Samsung TouchWiz, provide a different—and better—interface for adding shortcuts.

You can move apps around on the home screen by repeating the same procedure: Long-press the app's shortcut until you feel the vibration and then drag it to a new location.

Remember that your device will actually have more than one home screen—usually, either five or seven. You can move shortcuts to other screens by dragging the shortcuts to the edge, waiting for the next screen to appear, and then dropping them in place.

You can remove shortcuts from the home screen by pressing and holding and dragging the shortcut to the Trash Can, which will be on the Applications Bin's tab. If you uninstall an application, its shortcut is removed automatically.

ADDING APPLICATION SHORTCUTS TO YOUR HOME SCREENS IN HONEYCOMB

If you use a tablet that runs Honeycomb, you need to follow a different, but thankfully easier, method to add shortcuts to your home screens. To begin, open your Application Launcher by selecting the Apps icon in the top-right corner of the home screen. Then, long-press on an application you wish to add to the home screen. After about a second, a representation of your home screens will appear along the bottom of the Launcher (see Figure 3.1). Drag the icon for the app on the screen onto which you wish to add the shortcut and release.

ADDING WIDGETS TO YOUR HOME SCREEN

Many applications provide home screen widgets. A widget is essentially a miniature version of the application that runs directly from the home screen. Widgets can take up a lot of space on the home screen, or be the same size as an app shortcut. Either way, they provide instant access to the application's data.

Figure 3.1

Preparing to add a shortcut to a home screen in Honeycomb

You can add a widget to a home screen by long-pressing a blank area of the home screen. On Gingerbread and earlier versions of Android, a menu appears that includes the option to add widgets; select this option to bring up a list of all of the available applications that contain widgets. On Honeycomb, you will see a list of the available widgets along the bottom half of the screen (see Figure 3.2). Either way, simply select the desired widget to add it to your home screen.

Widgets can be removed in the exact same manner as application shortcuts: long-press the widget and drag it to the Trash Can.

ORGANIZE YOUR HOME SCREEN SHORTCUTS WITH FOLDERS

Folders enable you to organize your home screen, allowing you to place many more application shortcuts than might otherwise fit. Note that folders are not available in Honeycomb. You can create a folder by pressing and holding your finger on the home screen and then selecting Folders

TIDBIT

Devices running Motorola's version of Android include a set of Motorola widgets along with the Android widgets. Many of these widgets are actually quite useful. I'm particularly fond of the set of widgets that enable you to quickly toggle Wi-Fi, Bluetooth, GPS, and Airplane mode on and off; the Photo Slideshow is also pretty cool.

Figure 3.2

Selecting a widget in Honeycomb

from the menu that appears. Another menu appears, asking you to determine which kind of folder you want (see Figure 3.3). Select New Folder to create a new, blank folder on your home screen.

You can rename the folder by selecting the folder to open it and then pressing and holding again on the title bar of the folder. Applications can be added to the folder by dragging them onto its icon.

CHANGING THE WALLPAPER

Just as you have likely customized the background or wallpaper on your computer, you can change the wallpaper on your device as well. To get started, long-press on the home screen and select Wallpapers. You then can choose Live Wallpaper, Media Gallery (to select a specific photo), or Wall-

papers (to select a stock wallpaper). Alternately, you can press the Menu key while on the home screen, and select "Wallpapers."

Stock Wallpapers

Each device comes with a set of stock wallpaper art. My Droid X has 15 mostly dark, moody, and abstract wallpaper designs, while the LG Ally shipped with 33 wallpapers, most of them bright, happy landscapes. I suspect that these designs have as much to do with the target audience of the device as they do with any real design sense, although I am not sure what the Droid X's wallpapers say about me.

You can choose the wallpaper by selecting the Set Wallpaper button. This selection returns you to your home screen, where you will see the new wallpaper stretched across all of your screens (see Figure 3.4).

Figure 3.3
Preparing to add a folder

Figure 3. 4
The new wallpaper applied to the home screen

Media Gallery

Your Media Gallery stores all of your images and videos. The gallery is discussed in detail in Chapter 9; for now, we will just use it to set the wallpaper using your own image. If you do not have any images in the gallery yet, you might skip ahead and read Chapter 9 and then come back when you are done.

Using your own picture as the wallpaper involves selecting Media Gallery from the wallpaper options. The gallery opens, displaying all of the images currently stored on your SD card. Select the image you want to use and then crop it to the appropriate dimensions for the home screen. Select Save, and the picture is applied as the wallpaper.

Live Wallpapers

Live wallpapers are essentially animated backgrounds for your home screen. As with the stock wallpapers, each device that supports live wallpapers ships with a slightly different set. Several of the live wallpapers

ALTERNATE APP

Many additional live wallpapers are available in the Android Market. Simply search for "live wallpaper" to view the list. A few are free, but most cost between $1 and $2. The Market also contains a variety of apps that replace the home screen altogether and allow you a greater level of customization than what you find in the regular version.

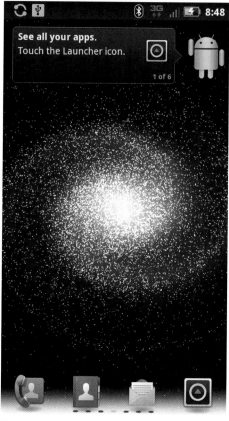

display waveforms based on the currently playing music track. The Droid X includes a Google Map live wallpaper that uses GPS to always display your current location. After you find the live wallpaper you want, click Set Wallpaper to apply it to the home screen (see Figure 3.5). You can download new Live Wallpapers from the Android Market. Note that older phones may not be able to run Live Wallpapers.

Figure 3.5
Live wallpaper applied to the home screen

The Phone

The Skim

Recently, I was cleaning out the kitchen junk drawer when I stumbled across our old address book. Flipping through it made me chuckle, as it was littered with addresses that had to be scribbled out and replaced as friends and family moved, and even entire entries crossed out for some now long-forgotten reason. Of course, it was also hopelessly disorganized; yes, the "a" names were under A, but they were in an essentially random order after that. The entire book was also absolutely useless, since it was sitting, buried, in the back of the junk drawer as we had long since stopped using it, having transferred all of those addresses and phone numbers to the computer and now, to our phones.

ADDING CONTACTS

Your mobile device includes a powerful contact manager. Most people make most of their calls to a select group of people: friends, family, and co-workers. Although prior generations actually had to remember the phone numbers of the people they wanted to call, your phone now can remember them for you, leaving you more memory for random Monty Python quotes and the like.

Because your Android device is synched with your Google account, you may find that you have contacts immediately upon setting up your phone, as any contacts you have in your Gmail account are imported. If you are using a mobile carrier that relies on SIM cards, such as T-Mobile or AT&T, your contact from your previous phone likely also are imported.

Whether you begin with many contacts or have a completely empty contact list, you can begin adding new contacts right away, directly on your phone. Begin by opening the Contacts application, which can be found in the Applications Bin. You also can open Contacts by either selecting the Call button on the home screen or by pressing the call button, if your phone has one.

After you are in your Contacts application, press your phone's Menu button and select Add Contact or New Contact, depending on your model (see Figure 4.1). Enter any or all of the information for the contact. If you plan to use the contact for

Figure 4.1

The Contact application's menu

TIP

If you want a particular contact to appear at the top of your contact list, add a space to the beginning of the name. In Figure 4.1, note that the first contact in my list is Home. It shows up there, rather than down with the other H contacts, because there is actually a space before the H, which causes the list to think that it should be alphabetized with the other contacts that start with nonalphabetic characters.

calls, then you will need to enter at least a name and a phone number. You can specify multiple numbers for each contact and set whether the number is for work, mobile, home, or any other custom type. If you have a picture of the person on your phone, you can also add the picture to the contact, which will display both in the Contact list and as caller ID when that person calls you or call him.

At the bottom of the Add Contact screen, select Additional Info or More to display more fields. The contact application enables you to enter birthday and anniversary dates, both of which are added to your calendar so that you do not forget them. Most Android devices provide fields for nicknames and websites for the person.

Each contact can have its own custom ringtone, so that you can tell who is calling without even looking at your phone. When adding the contact, select Ringtone and then select a ringtone from the list that appears. You also can use music you have uploaded to your phone as your contact's ringtone; see Chapter 8 for more information.

MANAGING CONTACTS ON YOUR COMPUTER

All of your device's contacts are automatically synchronized online via your Google account, meaning that you can manage contacts in either location. Sometimes, using your computer may be easier, particularly if your device has only a small on-screen keyboard.

Managing your contacts online involves going to www.gmail.com and logging in, using the same username and password you used when you initially set up the computer. After you log into Gmail, click Contacts on the left. You can click a contact in the list to bring up the details, which will match those on your phone.

ORGANIZING CONTACTS INTO GROUPS

Scrolling through a long list of contacts every time you need to find someone can be time-consuming. Android enables you to group your contacts into smaller lists so that they are more manageable. From your Contacts list, press the button near the top of the screen that looks like two heads., then click the green Plus sign. Enter a name for your

TIP

If you have a contact for which you need to dial a number, wait a few seconds, and then dial an extension, you can add pauses into the number by entering commas between the number and the extension. Each comma adds a two-second pause. For example, if you needed to dial 555-1212, wait four seconds, and then dial extension 123, you could enter the number as 555-1212,,123.

group and select OK. Select the check box next to any contact you want to add to the group and then select Done (see Figure 4.2).

Each contact can be added to as many groups as you want, so for example, a co-worker who is also a friend might be in both a Work group and a Friends group.

ALTERNATE APP

Many alternate contact applications exist in the Market, but one of the nicer ones is aContacts. This contact replacement displays your contacts in a picture-oriented interface, so if you have pictures associated with many of your contacts, you can pick that contact from a grid of pictures rather than a list of names. This app also enables you to set up multiple ways to contact people, including integration with social networking sites such as Facebook and Twitter.

TIP

If you use Outlook or another desktop e-mail program, you can very easily import your existing contacts into Gmail. You need to export the contact list from the program. The actual steps to do so will vary from one program to the next and even, in the case of Outlook at least, from one version to the next, but you should be able to find instructions online. Just make sure that you export the list in CSV format, or comma-separated values. Then from your Gmail contacts, click Import Contacts, select the exported file, and click Import. I recently went on a vacation with my family, and we discovered that we could not send postcards because several other family addresses were stuck at home in Outlook. Now that I have imported my Outlook contacts into Gmail, I never need to worry about that again.

Figure 4.2

Adding members to the group

After you have your groups created, you can access them by selecting the same two-headed-icon you used to initially access the screen from which you created the group.

You can also create and manage your groups in Gmail on your computer. When viewing your contacts, you will see a list of your groups on the left side of the page. Clicking any of these groups displays its members. When in a group, you can click the Add to Group button at the top of the page and type the name of a contact you want to add. When you are viewing the Detail page for a contact, you can click Groups at the top of the page to view a list of your available groups and select the check box next to a group name to add the contact

to it. On the main page of the contact list, the group to which a contact belongs is displayed on the far-right side of the page.

CALLING A CONTACT

You can select any contact to display its details. From there, select the small green phone icon to place the call. You also can long-press a contact in the contact list and select Call Contact from the menu that appears.

If your phone has a dedicated Call button, you can press it to go directly into the dialer. If you do not have a Call button, you can select the phone icon from your home screen to place a call directly. In the dialer, you can select Contacts to view your list, then select the picture or icon next to the contact's name, and select the green phone icon to place the call (see Figure 4.3).

If you have stored multiple numbers for a contact, you will be asked which number you want to call when you select the contact.

MANUALLY DIALING NUMBERS

Although most of the calls you place likely will be to your contacts, of course, sometimes need to directly dial a number. Either press your phone's call button or select the phone icon on the home screen to launch the Dialer application. From there, select Dialer to display a normal phone keypad, and type the number you want to call. Select the green phone icon to connect (see Figure 4.4).

As you enter the number, the Dialer will attempt the match the number to those stored in your Contacts. If it finds a match, you can stop dialing and select the contact instead.

USING FAVORITES

Those numbers that you call most frequently can be added to your Favorites list for easy access. You can call a Favorite directly by selecting the green phone icon.

To add a contact to your Favorites, long-press the contact's name on the Contact list and then choose Add to Favorites. Likewise, if someone has fallen out of favor, you can long-press the contact on the Favorites list and select Remove from Favorites. While viewing a contact's details, you can tap the small star icon to the right of the

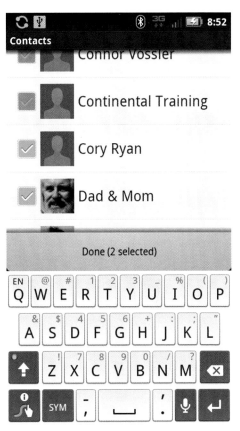

Figure 4.3
Calling a contact from the dialer

contact's name to add that contact to your favorites.

SPEED DIAL

Not all Android devices support speed dial, instead relying on Favorites to provide quick access to frequently used contacts, but some devices do have this long-standard feature. From the Dialer application, press the Menu button and select Speed Dial Setup. Next, select Add Speed Dial, and then select the contact.

When set up, you can go to the dialer and long-press the appropriate speed dial

TIDBIT

Motorola includes additional home screen widgets on most of its phones. One of the more useful is the Contact quick tasks, which adds a widget personalized for a contact. The widget displays the contact's picture and can be customized to show up to four ways to connect to the contact, either via multiple phone numbers or multiple numbers to send text messages. After the contact is associated with the widget and the numbers entered, you can enable one-touch dialing so that you can select the widget and directly place a call. HTC Sense phones include a home screen widget that shows your favorite contacts.

Figure 4.4

Manually dialing a number

number to connect. Honestly, although people have relied on speed dial to quickly reach contacts for years, in Android you probably can call a contact as quickly by going to your Favorites as you can by going to the Dialer, and using Favorites does not require that you memorize which contact is associated with which number, so this is not really all that exciting a feature. If you have a phone that does not support speed dialing, you are unlikely to miss it.

Whether or not your phone supports speed dial, all Android devices enable you to add a shortcut to your home screen to directly dial a number. To add one, long-press on the home screen. Select Shortcuts and then Contact or Direct Dial.

USING THE RECENT LIST

Your phone's Recent list shows the most recent calls you have placed or received (see

Figure 4.5). The number of calls listed in the list will vary from one device to the next. Although there are easier ways to connect to your contacts, the list is useful to return missed calls or call back to a number that you manually dialed.

An even more useful feature of the list is the capability to add new contacts from it. If someone calls you, and you want to add that person to your list, you can long-press the number and then select Add to Contacts. From there, you have the option to either add the number to a new or an existing contact. If you select New, you are taken to the

Figure 4.5
The Recent list

manual dialer and select the Voice Dial icon. Speak the name of the contact you want to call.

Of course, the steps required to get into the voice dialer pretty much defeat its purpose, so for added safety, you can add a shortcut to the home screen. Many phones include a Voice Commands application that enable you a considerable amount of control over your phone by talking to it. Launch the application and then say "Call Home" or something similar (see Figure 4.6).

If your phone has a physical Call button, you have even easier access to the Voice Dialer: Press and hold the Call button for about 4 seconds, and you should see the Voice Dialer appear.

CALLING FROM THE BROWSER

One of Android's nicest features is the way in which the phone functionality integrates with the web browser. I cannot honestly recall the last time it even occurred

Add Contact page, where the number will be filled in for you.

If you want to clear the list and remove the history of calls, you can press the Menu key and then select Clear List.

VOICE DIALING

You can use voice dialing to place calls by talking to your phone. When you are driving, it is unsafe to be distracted while you find a contact or manually dial a number, so voice dialing enables you to keep your eyes on the road and still place the call. From the Dialer application, go to the

TIP

In order to effectively use voice dialing, you need to speak slowly and clearly. You also need to try to minimize background noise, so it may not be a terribly effective way to call someone from a crowded bar or rock concert. If you have a hands-free device, you can speak directly into its microphone, which is likely to be more effective than simply shouting in the general direction of the phone.

Calling...

Home

Home 1

8:58

Figure 4.6
Using the Voice Commands application to place a call

to me to look up a number in a physical phone book; instead, when I need to call a local business, I use Google on my phone to look up the business and then place the call directly from the web.

Launch your phone's browser from your Applications Bin or, if you have one, a shortcut on the home screen.

If you know the address of the website for the company or organization you are trying to reach, you can enter it directly; otherwise, search Google and then click the link to the site.

When on the site, look around for the phone number; most sites have a Contact or About Us page that lists this, although many will place it on the bottom of each page.

When you find the number, select it. This action opens the dialer with the number pre-entered, and you can press the Call button to place the call.

USING THE SPEAKER PHONE

While placing a call, you can turn on the speaker phone so that you do not have to hold the phone up to your ear. To enable the speaker phone select Speaker while the call is ringing or at any time during the call. Turn the speaker back off by pressing the same button. I find the speaker phone particularly useful when calling companies that are either entirely computer-driven, such as the monthly call I make to pay my mortgage electronically or when sitting on hold for an extended period of time. Note that the speaker is not an acceptable alternative to a hands-free device while driving, as you will need to hold the phone fairly close to your head in order to hear and be heard.

CONFERENCE CALLING

You can speak to more than one person at a time using conference calling. To use this feature, :place a call to the first person to whom you want to connect. Then while in that call, select Add Call. When the second call connects, select Merge Calls to connect the second call to the first (see Figure 4.7).

GOOGLE VOICE

Google Voice is the company's phone service. Google Voice gives you a dedicated phone number in an area code of

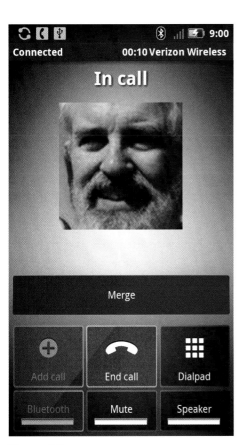

Merge

Add call   End call   Dialpad

Bluetooth   Mute   Speaker

Figure 4.7

Merging calls

TIP

You can do a local search on Google and likely get the company or organization's phone number without having to go to its site. In Google's search bar, type the name you want to search, followed by a city and state. For example, you could type "White House, Washington, DC." When the listing appears, you may see the number for the company directly on the Google results page, which you can click to go to the dialer. You can also search for people, although your results will vary. Be sure to spell their names correctly and include a city and state to increase your chances of finding them.

your Google Voice voice mail and accept Google's terms and privacy policy. After you have your PIN selected, the system prompts you to enter a phone number to which you want to forward Google Voice calls. Finally,

your choosing. The Google Voice number is attached to you, not to any particular device, and can be set up to ring multiple phones simultaneously.

You can request a Google Voice number by visiting www.google.com/voice and logging in with your Google account username and password. You then are prompted to search for an available phone number by entering either a desired area code, city, or ZIP code or a word or phrase to which you want to map the number. You then can select from a list of available numbers. Next, you need to enter a PIN to use for accessing

TIDBIT

The process outlined in this section on calling a number directly from the browser is in fact not limited to the browser. When you search for an address in the Google Maps application on your phone, you will often get the phone number at that address and will be able to tap it to place the call directly within Maps. Many other applications provide similar functionality.

you are shown a screen with a two-digit confirmation key. Press the Call Me Now button to have Google Voice call you; when you answer, enter the two-digit number. At this point, your Google Voice account is set up

After you have your Google Voice account set up, you can begin associating numbers such as your mobile device with it. That way, when someone calls your Google Voice number, the call is forwarded to your mobile.

Installing the Google Voice App on Your Phone

To fully use the features of Google Voice on your phone, you need to install the free Google Voice application, which you can get from the Android Market. Once installed, the application enables you to associate your Google Voice account with your device.

The next step is to decide which calls you want to make with Google Voice. You have four options: Use Google Voice to make all calls, do not use Google Voice for calling, only use Google Voice for international calls, and ask for each call. If you decide to use Google Voice to make calls, your Google Voice number appears as the caller ID for these calls, rather than your actual mobile number.

You also can use Google Voice as the voice mail provider for your phone, so that all calls are routed to the Google Voice Voicemail box instead of your regular voice mail. See the following section, "Google Voice Voicemail," for details on its advantages.

You also can enable a feature that sends you a text message whenever you get a call. Be aware that if you have a mobile plan with limited text messaging, you may not want to enable this feature.

Google Voice Voicemail

When someone calls your Google Voice number and you do not answer, he or she is transferred to your Google Voice Voicemail box. To your caller, the process is the same as any other voice mail. However, you have two options as to how to retrieve the voice mail message. You can call into Google Voice and listen to the message as normal, or you can read the message, thanks to Google Voice's transcription capabilities. Although the transcription is not always perfect, it will give you a good idea of what the message says. You can also view your voice mail box from any computer by logging into Google Voice in your browser.

Other Google Voice Features

You can set personalized voice mail greetings for your contacts in Google Voice, so you can have one outgoing message for business contacts and another for friends and family. To set up this feature, open the contact in your computer's browser, either through the Google Voice page or your Gmail contacts and click Edit Google Voice Settings.

You can use Google Voice to place international calls, usually at much cheaper rates than you will find elsewhere. You need to add credits to your Google Voice account in order to pay for these calls, which can be done from the Google Voice home page on your computer. You can place the call from your browser, which then rings through to your phone, or if you have the Google Voice application installed on your phone and have configured it to either make all calls or all international calls, you can dial the number directly.

Google Voice also can be set up to receive text messages. Whenever you receive a text, it appears in the texting application in your phone, and also in your Google Voice inbox. In addition, you can configure the system to send you an e-mail when you receive a text.

The Block Caller feature of Google Voice enables you to permanently prevent particular callers from reaching you. From your Google Voice inbox on your computer, you can click the More link and then select Block Caller. When that caller attempts to contact you again, he or she gets a message that your number has been disconnected or is no longer in service. It is particularly handy for those annoying solicitation calls.

Back in ancient times, people used their answering machines to screen callers—they would let the call go through to the machine, listen to the message, and then pick up the phone if it turned out that the caller was someone to whom they actually wanted to speak. Voice mail systems long ago removed this capability, but for better or worse, Google Voice gives it back to you. When a call comes in, you have the option of answering or sending the call to voice mail; if you chose the latter, you can listen as the message is left and press the star key to pick up. It is probably going to be fairly obvious that you were screening the call, though, so you might use this feature with caution.

Google Voice also enables you to send SMS, or text messages, via its service rather than your mobile providers. This essentially means that you can get around any charges your provider imposes for text messages you send.

TIP

Many calling plans today include a feature that enables you to add a limited set of numbers from which calls are always free. A creative use of Google Voice can potentially enable you to get essentially unlimited calling minutes each month: Add your Google Voice number to your free list and then give out your Google Voice number to your contacts rather than your actual mobile number. That way, almost all calls into your phone appear to be coming from the Google Voice number, and will, thus, be free.

21st Century Communication

The Skim

spent the summer after graduating high school as an intern for my congressman. Not only was that my first experience in an office, it also was my first experience with e-mail. Later that year, after settling into the residence halls in college, I was lucky to be one of the first people in the hall to get Internet access in my room and, along with it, another e-mail account, although it relied on a system known as Kermit that was, even at the time, rather primitive.

Little did I know that I was not just learning some new toy, but rather learning something that would, decades later, become my primary means of communication. Most of my business contacts today are over e-mail, and, in fact, I have had exactly one phone conversation with the people at Wiley, the publishers of this book. Although publishing obviously happened before the advent of e-mail, I am not sure I would even know how to do it.

Within the last few years, I have had another major shift in the way I communicate. I still rely on e-mail, but today, my primary means of reading and writing e-mail has shifted from my laptop and desktop machines to my mobile devices. Now, I only check messages on my computers when they include an attachment that I cannot open or edit on my phone or tablet, an event that is becoming, thankfully, quite rare.

SWITCHING TO GMAIL

In 2004, Google began issuing invitations to a special beta of its newest service, Gmail, which it was touting as a new way to work with e-mail. I do not recall precisely when I got my then-coveted invite, but I do remember my initial first impression of Gmail; mostly, it seemed to be yet another free e-mail service. As I already had e-mail, both personal and business, coming into Outlook and already was using a separate Yahoo account to monitor groups, I did not really see the value of Gmail.

You stopped needing an invitation to join Gmail in 2007; in 2009, the company finally removed the "beta" label from the service. Over the years, I maintained my Gmail account as a repository for spam, but checked it only once every few months.

That all changed when, quite suddenly, my laptop died. I still do not know exactly what happened, but whatever fried the motherboard took the hard drive with it. Thankfully, all of my important documents, including the book I was writing at the time, were backed up on my home desktop computer, but I had been lax in backing up my Outlook file, so when the laptop died, I lost about six months of important e-mail. As I need access to e-mail when I'm away from home, switching over to Outlook on the desktop until I replaced the laptop was not really feasible, and the company with whom I host my website and, by extension, my personal e-mail provides an online e-mail application that is horrible, to put it nicely.

All of these factors, along with the fact that as an Android user I knew that I could easily get Gmail on my phone forced me to, at long last, take a serious look at Gmail, and it took only about a day to realize how horribly, completely wrong I had been all those years. Gmail is, in fact, far more than "just another free e-mail service."

Signing Up with Gmail

If you do not already have a Gmail account, you can get one easily enough: Simply go to www.gmail.com and click Create an Account. However, as an Android user, you almost certainly already have a Google account, so you, in fact, have a Gmail account as well, so rather than creating a new account, you should instead sign in with your username and password.

Organizing E-mail

The most difficult thing about switching to Gmail from every other e-mail system I've used is getting used to Google's approach to e-mail organization. Outlook, along with every other desktop e-mail application, allows you to organize your e-mail into folders. Other free online e-mail systems such as Yahoo Mail follow the same model. In Gmail, however, you do not have folders. Really, all of your e-mail always simply resides in a mailbox. Instead, you use a concept known as labels to sort and filter your messages. The Inbox, in fact, is nothing more than one of those labels.

Creating New Labels

To create new labels in your Gmail account, click Labels, then select Manage Labels from the buttons along the top of your inbox. On the Settings page that appears, type a new label and click Create. Should you create a label that you decide you do not want, you can click the remove the link next to the label in question.

Manually Labeling Messages

You can apply a label to messages when they arrive in your inbox. Simply click the message to open it and then click the Labels drop-down and select the label you want to apply to the message (see Figure 5.1).

Automatically Labeling Messages

When I used Outlook, I relied on its Rules feature to automatically move incoming messages into appropriate folders. With Gmail, I can use Filters to the same affect;

TIP

One of the advantages of using labels in Gmail as opposed to the traditional folder-based approach of other systems is that any message may have multiple labels applied to it. If you have a message that might logically fall under several different categories, you would have to either pick a single one or create duplicate copies of the message when using folders. With Gmail's Labels feature, you can apply all of the matching labels to a message, in effect organizing it into multiple categories.

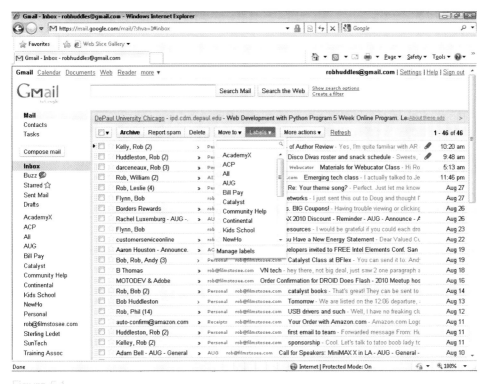

Figure 5.1

Adding a label to a message

incoming messages are automatically given appropriate labels. To create a filter, open a message that matches the criteria you want to use. and then click the small drop-down arrow next to the Reply button, and select Filter messages. A page will now open, allowing you to set up the criteria you want to use for the filter. The e-mail address of the person who sent the message will be automatically set, but you can add criteria or remove the address and filter based on something else. When you have the criteria set, click Next Step.

The next page enables you to set the action to be taken by the filter. Although you can apply actions such as marking messages as read or deleting messages, I tend to

use filters simply to apply labels. From the drop-down list of labels, select the one you want to use; you also can choose New Label to create a label on the fly. When the label is selected, seleck the Also apply this filter to the conversations below check box, and click Create Filter. From then on, messages matching the filter will have the appropriate label automatically applied when they arrive in your inbox.

Viewing Messages by Label

On your main inbox page, you will see a list of your labels to the left (see Figure 5.2). You can click on any of these labels to view all of the messages tagged with that label (see Figure 5.3). In effect, this is the same

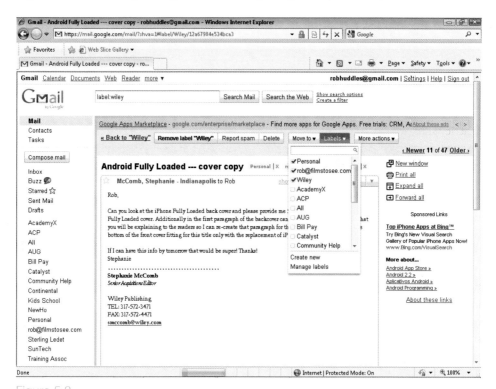

Figure 5.2

The list of labels on the inbox page

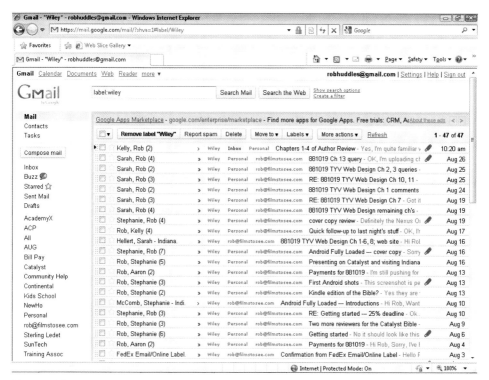

Figure 5.3

Messages under a particular label

functionality you had in your old e-mail system when you would view the messages in a folder, except with the important caveat that in Gmail, messages can have multiple labels, so a single message might appear under more than one label.

Archiving Messages

A recent trend being pushed by organizational experts is known as inbox zero. The idea is that you want to keep your inbox empty by either deleting or filing all messages as soon as they arrive. Achieving inbox zero involves a fairly obvious procedure in folder-based e-mail systems: Move each message you want to keep out of your inbox and into a folder. In Gmail, the solution is

less obvious but in many ways easier. As we have already seen, Gmail relies on labels to organize messages, but by default labeling a message does not remove it from the inbox view. Instead, you need to archive your messages. Archiving a message really does nothing more than remove the message from the inbox view. The message is not deleted. Instead, it will only show up when you view the messages for a particular label.

You can archive a message while reading it by simply clicking the Archive button at the top of the message's window. You can archive messages in bulk by clicking the check mark next to each message to be archived in the main inbox and then clicking the Archive button. Note that you can select a group of messages with different labels and archive them at once, something that you cannot do under traditional e-mail systems.

Note that archiving messages is useful even if you do not want to achieve inbox zero. One definite limitation of Gmail is that its web-based interface limits the number of message you can see at the same time, so if you have a lot of messages in your inbox, you may need to click the Next arrow button to see the next set. Archiving messages allows you to limit your inbox to only those very important messages you want to see at a glance. Note, however, there is an important difference between archiving and deleting. Archived messages remain in your mailbox, in the same way that a traditional e-mail program stores them in folders. Deleting messages removes them from the mailbox altogether, and deleted messages are permanently removed after 30 days.

Searching Mail

Google is, of course, primarily a search company, so you would rightfully expect its e-mail system to include a powerful search capability, and you will not be disappointed when using Gmail. The top of every page in the system includes a search box that allows you to search either your own mail or the web for particular terms. You can search for anything in the message, whether it is the sender's address or text in the body of the e-mail.

Spam

Ever since Gary Thuerk sent the first unsolicited e-mail in 1978, spam has been an unfortunate fact of modern life. According to Wikipedia, an estimated 200 billion spam messages were being sent every day

in August 2010, and that number is likely growing. All e-mail systems include some sort of spam filtering, but in all my years of being online and using e-mail, I have never worked with a system that filters messages as effectively as Gmail. In Outlook, I had my spam setting at its maximum, meaning that although almost no actual spam got through to my inbox, a lot of legitimate messages got marked as spam. This meant that I had to check my spam folder constantly for these false positives. The irony, of course, is that this meant that I still needed to look at all of my spam.

Since switching to Gmail, I have gotten almost no spam. No e-mail system will ever be absolutely perfect in spam detection, so "almost no spam" is the best one can hope for. The real beauty of Gmail, though, is that I also have almost no false positives. I've gone from checking my spam folder several times a day to essentially never checking it at all. As I wrote this, I went ahead and looked in my spam folder just to verify that I was not lying. I currently have 486 spam messages there, and although I am not going to go through every one of them, I can say that none that has arrived in the last week is a false positive. That is a far, far better percentage than I have seen on any other system, and yet another reason why I wonder why it took me so long to switch over to Gmail.

Importing Your Other Accounts

An initial concern when switching to Gmail was my desire to keep my old e-mail account, which I have had for more than a decade. Fortunately, you can quite easily import almost any e-mail account to Gmail so that messages sent to it will appear in your inbox alongside any messages e-mailed to you directly at your gmail.com address.

To import other e-mail accounts, click the Settings link in the top-right corner of any page in Gmail and then select Accounts and Import. About halfway down this page, you will find a button labeled Add POP3 e-mail account. Click this button to launch the Import Wizard. You will need to provide the e-mail address you want to import, and your username, password, and server for the account. If you do not know any of these details, you can ask your Internet service provider or your company's IT department for help.

ACCESSING GMAIL ON YOUR DEVICE

One of the biggest reasons to switch to Gmail as your primary source of e-mail is its close integration with Android devices. The Gmail application comes preinstalled on your device, and, in fact, the process of configuring your device and synching it to your Google account when you first purchased it completed the setup process for the e-mail. All you need to do is launch the program to start receiving e-mail (see Figure 5.4).

Viewing Your Inbox

Gmail on your device works almost exactly the same way as Gmail on your computer. As messages come in, you see an icon appear in your Notifications Bar. Slide the Notifications Bar down to see details. If you have only a single unread message, the sender and first bit of the message will appear, but if you have more than one, you will see an indication of how many messages you have in that account. Select the notification to go to the Gmail application,

TIP

Many larger corporations use Microsoft Exchange Server, which uses a system known as IMAP for sending e-mail, rather than the more common POP3. Gmail may be able to import messages from Exchange or other IMAP-based systems, but you will need to test it to be sure. Some organizations also may intentionally block third-party systems such as Gmail from accessing their servers, so it is possible that you will be unable to import your corporate mail. Thankfully, you may still be able to check your corporate e-mail on your device, which will be discussed in "Getting Other E-mail on Your Device" later in this chapter.

TIDBIT

One of the really great features of Honeycomb is the addition of scrollable widgets, which are particularly useful with mail. I have widgets for both my Gmail and my corporate e-mail on my Xoom home screen, and in both cases I can scroll through the messages directly on the home screen without having to open the apps themselves. There is nothing you need to do to get this to work: If the widget supports scrolling, it will scroll.

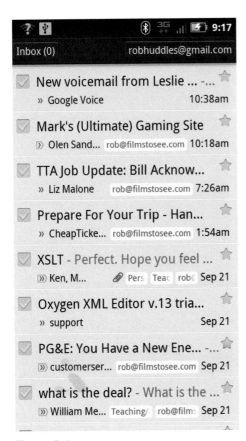

Figure 5.4

The preinstalled, preconfigured Gmail application

Forward buttons, either at the top or bottom of the message, depending on the version of Gmail your device is running. Selecting either Reply or Reply to all will bring up a new message screen, enabling you to enter your response while displaying the original e-mail (see Figure 5.5). Selecting Forward likewise displays a new message, with the added necessary To field highlighted. In either case, your on-screen keyboard should appear automatically unless your device has a physical keyboard. When you finish entering your response or the forwarding address, select either Send to send the mes-

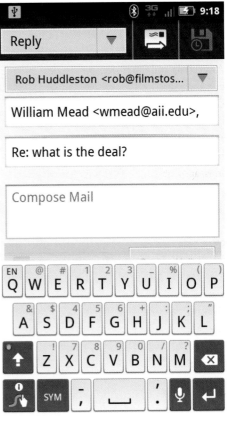

Figure 5.5

Replying to a message

which takes you directly to the first unread message. After reading, you can select one of the three buttons at the bottom to either archive or delete the message or go to the next oldest message in your inbox. You also can archive, label, or delete multiple messages at a time by selecting the check box next to the message and then selecting the appropriate option.

Replying and Forwarding

If you want to reply to the message or forward it, you will see Reply, Reply to all, and sage immediately, Save as draft to continue working on it later, or Discard if you change your mind about sending it at all.

Viewing HTML E-mail

Often, you receive messages that contain formatting and images. Your Gmail application automatically displays formatting in the message, but not images. This is done to speed up the rendering of complex e-mails on slower connections, but at any time, you can select the Show pictures button at the top of the message to view images along with the e-mail.

Viewing Messages by Label

As was discussed earlier, Gmail relies on labels rather than folders for organization. Any labels and filters you have set up on your computer are visible and accessible on your device. From your main inbox, you can press the Menu key on your device and then select View labels to see a list of all of the labels you have configured. Select a label to view the messages labeled with it (see Figure 5.6).

Composing Mail

When you need to send a new message, click the Menu button on your device, then select Compose from the options that appear. Enter the address of the person to whom you want to send the message, the subject, and the body, and then select Send. You can also select Save as draft if you need to interrupt writing the message or Discard if you change your mind about sending the message.

GETTING OTHER E-MAIL ON YOUR DEVICE

While Gmail is probably the easiest e-mail system to use on your device, you

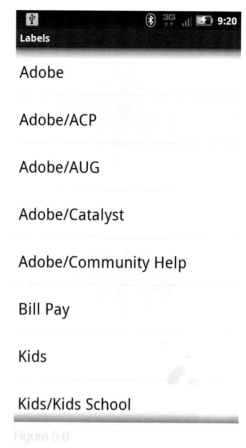

Figure 5.6

Viewing messages for a particular label

are by no means limited to it. (In fact, most devices don't even have the Gmail app on the main home screen by default.) In addition to the Gmail application, your device comes preinstalled with another application, simply called Email. Using this application requires a few additional steps to set up. After launching the application, press the device's Menu button, then select Manage accounts. On the next screen, select Add account, and then Email. Enter the e-mail address and your password for the account you want to use, and select

TIDBIT

Prior to getting the Droid X, I would have recommended against anyone seriously trying to compose more than extremely simple e-mails on their phones. Even with a physical keyboard, typing long messages was inefficient at best. That has all changed now, however, and not due to anything inherent about the Droid X but rather, because of Swype. If you have Swype available on your device for text input, I cannot recommend it enough, and if you skipped over the part in Chapter 1 that discussed how to enable and use it, I also would suggest that you go back and reread it, since honestly it is about the single coolest thing on your device.

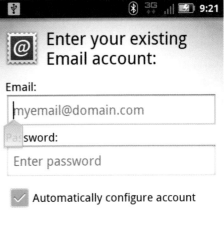

Figure 5.7

Entering your username and password

Next (see Figure 5.7). After that, one of two things will happen: Either the account will be set up and be ready to use, or, more likely, you will get a message saying that the account cannot be set up automatically and that you need to manually configure it.

When you need to manually configure the account, you are presented with four categories: General Settings, Incoming Server, Outgoing Server, and Other Settings. The General Settings screen will contain a name for the account, your name, and your e-mail account. The incoming server settings are one of the two places where you will likely need to make some configuration changes. At the top of the screen, set the type to the appropriate value; if you are using corporate e-mail, it likely needs to be changed from POP mail server to IMAP. Make sure that the server address is correct; contact your

IT department if you are unsure what the server address is. The port is the really technical bit here; this is another setting you need to just check with your IT department. Double-check your username and password, and again ask IT whether you need a secure connection and certificate verification. The outgoing server settings are similar to the incoming and are mostly things that you will again need to verify with your IT staff.

After you complete the setup, you should see a message letting you know that the setup was successful and that you can now access your e-mail. Tap Done. You should then be taken to the e-mail application where you can view, reply, and manage your e-mail.

INSTANT MESSAGING

Instant messaging has long been an effective way for people to keep in touch on their computers. IM, or chat, allows you to communicate in real time with one or more others. Initially, chat systems suffered from a limitation whereby users could chat with other users only on the same system. If you wanted to chat with one friend who used only AOL's chat and another who relied on the MSN system, you would have to download and install two separate chat programs, one for each system. Today, many applications exist to allow you to chat on multiple systems at once, thus removing this limitation.

Thanks to several free applications available on Android, you can now take your chatting with you wherever you go. However, your device also should have included the Google Talk application, which has the ability to connect to multiple accounts. To launch Talk, simply open your Application tray and select its icon.

When you first launch Talk, your Google contacts that also use the Google chat service will be displayed. You can see each contact's status, and begin chatting with any who currently are available by simply selecting his name (see Figure 5.8).

You can add connections by pressing your device's Menu button and selecting Add friend. This selection opens a screen into which you can enter an e-mail address of the person with whom you want to chat and then send that person an invitation. After your friend receives and approves the invitation, he will be added to your contact list.

ALTERNATE APP

Unlike its competitors, Android enables developers to create applications that directly compete with or supplant the built-in applications, and e-mail is no exception. One very popular alternate e-mail application is K-9, which offers improved controls over features such as how often messages are pulled from the server and the number of messages to display.

TIP

When setting up your e-mail, you need to decide whether you want to delete the messages from the server or leave them. If you plan to rely on your device as a secondary e-mail application, but still want to use Outlook or some other desktop application as your primary e-mail client, then make sure that you specify that your device should not delete messages as it pulls them down. Be aware that the reverse also can cause issues: If you have your desktop client delete messages from the server as it retrieves them—which is a common and often default setting—then you will not be able to also get those messages on your device.

Figure 5.8

Chatting with a contact

TEXTING

Texting was introduced fairly early in the development of mobile phones. Depending on your age, you likely either love or loathe texting, but even older users often can find it a useful means of communication—I receive at least as many texts from my dad as I do from anyone else. Of course, early phones had a significant limitation on texting, as typing messages on a phone's dialer was annoying, to say the least. Typing the word "hello" on a traditional 10-key pad requires 13 keypresses: 44-33-555-555-666.

Although some were able to learn to type longer messages quite quickly, most limited their messages or refused to adopt texting altogether because it was simply too difficult to type.

Your Android phone, of course, removes this limitation altogether, because whether it has a real keyboard or a virtual on-screen one, you have the full set of keys to work with, so typing "hello" is back to requiring only five keypresses. Even better, if your phone supports Swype, it is really one press-and-drag action.

Sending Texts

Your phone should have a texting or SMS application built in. Sending a text is as easy as launching the application, selecting New text message, and then typing the name of the contact to whom you want to send the message. Watch your phone as you type, as it will offer suggestions of the contacts, so you should not need to type the entire name. You also can enter a phone number if you need to send a message to someone not in your contact list.

After entering the contact, tap in the message section to type your message. Be aware that the SMS system limits messages to 160 characters. Most phones these days allow you to send messages of any length, but longer messages likely are split. If you do not have an unlimited texting plan, this can result in a single message being counted as several against your plan or, if you are over your limit, result in multiple charges per message.

Receiving Texts

When someone texts you, you will see an icon in your Notifications Bar and hear your default notification sound. Pull the Notifications Bar down to see who sent the message; select the message to read the full text. From there, you can type out a reply or press the Menu button and then delete to remove the message.

SOCIAL NETWORKING

Social networking has become an important part in many people's lives. Whether you use it to reconnect to old friends or keep in touch with business associates, social networking allows even the most homebound to maintain relationships.

The two biggest social networks today are Facebook and Twitter, and your Android device allows you to use both. Of course, you can use your device's browser to view either of them via their web interfaces, but a variety of applications on your device make the process much easier.

Facebook

As of July 2011, more than 750 million people were using Facebook, including an estimated 42% of the U.S. population. As of this writing, it is believed to be the second-most visited site on the web. From keeping up with the latest news from family members to playing social games, Facebook has become one of the primary motivators for many people to be online.

The Facebook application gives you many of the primary features of the site directly on your device. Some Android devices ship with the application preinstalled, but if yours did not, you can find it, free of charge, in the Market.

When you first launch the application, you will be presented with a log-in screen. Enter your e-mail address and password—

TIDBIT

Although your chat application will allow you to connect to multiple IM systems at the same time, you still need an account on each system in order to actually send or receive messages. Thankfully, all of these accounts are free, so while there will be some initial annoyance in connecting to a new friend who uses a system on which you are not yet registered, it should take only a few minutes to sign up. You also gain additional geek street cred when you belong to dozens of systems, so there's an advantage there as well.

ALTERNATE APP

The application mentioned previously is one of many available chat systems. You might also want to look at Meebo, available in the Android Market. Meebo includes many features not available in Talk. Talk's biggest disadvantage is that you must send an invitation to anyone with whom you want to chat, even if you previously had connected with that person in another chat application. Meebo, on the other hand, connects directly to the various chat services, so you will have instant access to any friends lists that you already have established.

TIP

Of course, you need to be careful when texting, as many mobile carriers impose significant costs on the practice. Most offer a plan with unlimited texting, but if you chose a different plan, you likely are limited on the number of texts you can send and receive before the bill starts going up. One friend of mine recently reported that her then-12-year-old daughter sent more than 18,000 text messages in a single month. Thankfully for all involved, the family had an unlimited texting plan, as otherwise their phone bill likely would have been in the thousands of dollars.

ALTERNATE APP

Although the default SMS application is serviceable, other alternatives do exist. Of particular note are chompSMS and Handcent SMS. chompSMS includes a fully customizable interface and the ability to create shortcuts for commonly texted words. Handcent SMS is likewise extremely customizable and has a Batch mode to send or delete multiple messages at once. Google Voice, which is discussed in detail in Chapter 4, can also serve as a text messaging application.

the same credentials you use to log into Facebook on the web—to connect. Your News Feed page loads as soon as you log in (see Figure 5.9).

From any page in the application, use your device's Back button to access the application's main page. This main page displays links to the seven sections of the application, along with pictures recently posted by your contacts. Select Profile to view and edit your personal profile, write on your wall, or access your Facebook photos.

Figure 5.9
The News Feed page

Returning to the main page, the Friends link displays your list of friends. You can select the link for any friend to be taken to his profile page. The search box at the top of the screen allows you to quickly filter the list to find a particular friend.

The Photos link on the main page displays your Facebook photo gallery. The camera icon at the top of the screen launches your device's camera application, enabling you to take and upload a picture directly to Facebook; see Chapter 9 for more details on using this feature.

The Events link displays your Facebook calendar. Although this is a feature of the Facebook website, I honestly never knew it was there until I used the Android application. In this case, the calendar is removing any excuses I might have had when forgetting someone's birthday.

From the main page, you can click Messages to view any messages that have been sent to you, view updates from Facebook, and see messages that you sent to your friends.

If you want to update your status, you can select the icon at the top of the main page. This will take you back to the News Feed page and allow you to write your update.

Facebook Widgets

The Facebook application allows you to install several widgets on your home screen. These include a simple widget that displays the most recent post to your News Feed and allows you to quickly post your own updates, as well as a Facebook Phonebook folder that gives you a quick way to call any of your Facebook friends who have added their phone numbers to their Facebook profile. See Chapter 3 for details on

TIDBIT

SMS stands for "Short Message Service." Although many think of texting as a relatively new phenomenon, it has been around for quite some time — it evolved from the radio telegraphy signals used in pagers, and the standards devices use to send and receive messages were adopted in 1985, although the first text message actually was sent on December 3, 1992. The idea of keeping messages short—the standard limits messages to 160 characters—was adopted because the original idea was to transmit the messages on otherwise-unused portions of the cell phone's signal. This allowed SMS to be supported instantly across the mobile space, so unlike modern technologies with 3G where available infrastructure often lags behind the user's desire to adopt, the SMS networks essentially already existed by the time anyone started using it. Today, texting is a massive industry, accounting by some estimates to close to $100 billion in revenue to carriers, in large part because although carriers charge customers to send and receive texts, the cost to the carrier for sending the messages is essentially zero.

adding widgets and folders to your home screen.

Twitter

Twitter is a social network with an interesting twist: All messages or status updates on the system can be no more than 140 characters in length. Thus, it encourages, or

TIDBIT

Unfortunately, as of this writing there was not an official Facebook app optimized for Honeycomb tablets. To access Facebook on your tablet, you will either need to use the web browser or a third-party app such as Friendcaster. Several other app vendors, including Friendster and Tweetdeck, provide the ability to access at least portions of Facebook's content through their apps as well.

TIDBIT

To many users, the most important aspect of Facebook is the games, such as Farmville and Mafia Wars. The Facebook application does not yet directly support feeding your Farmville habit, although future versions might. However, many of the games, including Mafia Wars, can be played via your device's browser. Simply go to the browser, navigate to Facebook. com, sign in, and play as usual. Other games such as Farmville, however, rely on Adobe Flash, and so you may or may not be able to play them on your device. See Chapter 11 for details on whether or not your device currently supports Flash player.

some might say forces, its users to post only short, concise messages.

Dozens of applications exist to allow you to use Twitter on your Android device. My favorite is Tweetdeck, an adaptation of a popular desktop-based Twitter client.

You can sign up for Twitter for free by either visiting www.twitter.com on your browser in either your computer or your device, or you can sign up for the service directly through Tweetdeck.

After you have an account, you need people to follow. Tweetdeck enables you to search for others on Twitter and then follow them. You can search by either Twitter username or, if the user included it in her profile, real name. For example, you can find me by either searching for my Twitter username, robhuddles, or by my real name. When you find someone you want to follow, simply select the Follow button on that person's profile page (see Figure 5.10), and you will begin receiving "tweets" or updates in what is known as your timeline.

Thanks to the enforced brevity of tweets, you will be able to read the entirety of each message in your timeline. Frequently, however, tweets will include pictures or links to websites. In these cases, you can choose the message to view it in its own window. If a picture is referenced in the tweet, you can view it. If it included a link, you can select the link to open the relevant page in your browser.

Social networks work only if they are a two-way street. Some of the people you follow will decide to follow you back; others will find you by looking through the lists of people following those that they follow. You should contribute to the community by posting tweets that will be read by your fol-

Figure 5.10

Following someone on Twitter

ALTERNATE APP

Another extremely popular Twitter client is Seesmic, which supports many of the same features as Tweetdeck, including support for multiple accounts and a companion desktop application.

TIP

Twitter traditionally has had a very low adoption rate. Estimates are that less than one-third of those who sign up for the service actually use it regularly. Although I have had many friends and family members sign up, few have adopted Twitter and continue to use it. I almost joined that statistic: I did not start using the service heavily until about six months after I first joined. Part of the problem, I think, is that the design and layout of Twitter.com—most people's starting point—is truly horrible and a definite barrier to adoption. The other, I believe more important factor, is finding the right people to follow. That is what it did for me: For those first six months, I was following a bunch of people who were, frankly, not interesting to me. I did not get hooked on Twitter until I found several real-world friends who used it as an effective communication tool and then, through them, found many others to follow who were regularly posting updates that I found interesting. So, if the service does not grab you initially, give it time and try to find those key people to follow who will make it interesting to you.

lowers. You can post these tweets by selecting the Update button at the bottom of the Tweetdeck window.

Type your post—remember that it must be no more than 140 characters—and select Send. The counter to the left of the button lets you know how many characters you have left. You will need to get used to the short character count, but after using the service for a while, you will get used to it.

Replying to Tweets

If you want to reach out to someone you follow, you can target a message directly

TIDBIT

Strictly speaking, your tweets cannot contain images. Instead, you can upload an image to one of the many free services that exist to support Twitter images and then include a link to the image in your tweet. If you use a service recognized by Tweetdeck, such as Twitpic, then your image automatically will appear in the application. Otherwise, your followers will be able to click the link in the tweet and view the image in the browser.

Website addresses often can be quite long and can take up most or all of your 140-character limit. Therefore, most users who post links to Twitter use a URL-shortening service such as bit.ly, which takes a long URL and converts it into a much shorter version. Because users will not be able to see the actual link, you always should include a description of the page to which you are linking in your tweet. The desktop version of Tweetdeck includes automatic URL shortening, but as of this writing, the Android application does not, so you will need to use your device's browser to go to bit.ly or one of the other services and shorten URLs, which you can then paste into your tweet.

at that person by beginning the post with the @ symbol and his or her username. For example, you can send me a message by posting to @robhuddles. These tweets will appear in your target's timeline and be visible to anyone who follows both of you, but also will appear in a separate column in Tweetdeck. The columns are not readily visible as the application is optimized to fit

on the small screen, but you can swipe the application window to the left to see your Replies column and view these posts. You also can reply to a user you follow by selecting one of his or her posts in your timeline.

Sending a Direct Message

You can send a message to another user, and only that user, by typing the letter D, followed by a space and his or her username. For example, you could direct message or DM me with d robhuddles. The difference between replies and direct messages is that any user who follows both you and the recipient will see replies, but only the recipient sees direct messages. However, in order to help prevent spam, Twitter imposes a special limit on direct messages: You can send only a DM to a user who you follow and who follows you back. Therefore, if you follow me and I follow you, we can DM one another, but if you are one of the million or so followers of a celebrity such as Adam Savage of the TV show *Mythbusters*, you cannot direct message him. By the way, Savage, who's Twitter username is @dont-trythis, is well worth following.

Retweeting

An important aspect of building the Twitter community is having users share information posted by other users, a process known a retweeting. You can take any message on your timeline and select it to view the details. Then select the Retweet button. You can edit the message and then select Send to post a copy of the original message to your timeline. The idea here is that while I might follow Star Trek's Wil Wheaton, you might not, so when he posts something I find interesting, I can retweet it. Now, even though you do not follow Wheaton, you will see what he posted through me. You can view the post and enjoy his wit or wisdom, and it might, and in the case of Wheaton should, encourage you to go ahead and start following him. Wheaton's Twitter name, by the way, is @wilw.

Unfollowing Users

You might, for a variety of reasons, choose to stop following someone. Tweet-deck makes the process easy: Simply select a tweet from a user, and then select his user-name. You will see a page that displays the profile of that user and includes an unfollow button: the button with the person and the small "x". Simply select this button to stop following. In case you are worried about offending someone, users are not informed when others stop following them.

Facebook Integration

Tweetdeck integrates Facebook and other social networks into your timeline. Each network's items are displayed using a dif-ferent color. You can add these networks by pressing the Menu button, then Accounts, and then selecting the plus sign next to each network (see Figure 5.11). Enter the account information for that network, and you will begin seeing its updates.

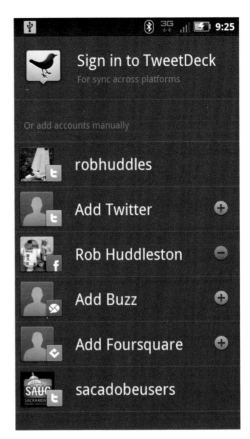

Figure 5.11

Adding social networks

Managing Your Time

The Skim

Google Calendar ◦ To-Do List ◦ Alarm Clock

hen I quit my last full-time job and became an independent contractor, I knew that I needed an effective way to keep track of my schedule. Of particular importance was the ability to have a calendar that I could access anywhere, anytime. I also needed something that would be easy to use and require little or no setup. As I was just embarking on a new career and facing somewhat uncertain finances, whatever I ended up using needed to be free. Thankfully, I quite quickly found a solution that met all of those criteria: Google Calendar.

GOOGLE CALENDAR

Google Calendar's web-based interface ensured I could get to it easily, and as I began to explore its features I realized it offered even more advantages. Years later, Android's built-in integration with Google Calendar was a major selling point for me, as the phone would allow me to have true anywhere access to my schedule. As with other Google services, the calendar is free. You can access it online by simply going to www.google.com/calendar.

Using the Google Calendar on Your Computer

Before you take a look at the calendar on your device, I would like to spend some time showing you some of the key features of the calendar on your computer. This way, you can get an idea of how you can manage your time whether you are at your computer or on your device.

Viewing the Calendar

Your default calendar requires no setup: Simply go to the calendar page when you are logged into Google and you will see it. Like other calendar applications, you have a variety of views to use to see your calendar. You can switch between these views using the buttons in the top-right corner of the screen (see Figure 6.1). You can view the calendar by day, by week, or by month. You also have an option of viewing four days at a time, which is a view very similar to the weekly

but easier to work with on smaller screens, and in a list-style Agenda view.

Navigating the Calendar

The buttons in the top-left corner of the calendar allow you to navigate. In any view, you can use the arrow buttons to move back and forth; how far you move depends on the view, so the right arrow moves you ahead one day in the Day view, but one month in the Month view. At any point, you can click the Today button to return to, well, today.

To the left of the calendar itself, you see a monthly grid displayed at all times. You can click on any day to jump there, use the arrows in this calendar to move forward or back

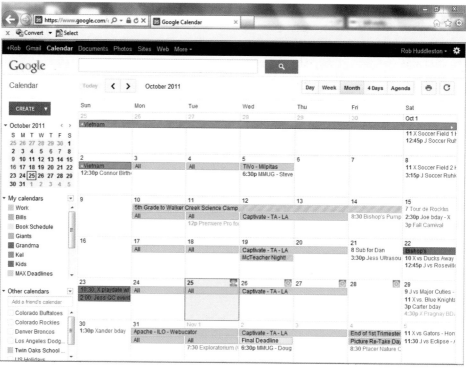

Figure 6.1

Use the buttons in the top-right corner to change how you view the calendar. Shown here is the Month view.

through the months, or click directly on the name of the month to switch to Month view.

If you have a mouse with a scroll wheel, you can use it to navigate as well. While your mouse pointer is over the main calendar, scrolling up moves you backward in time, and scrolling down moves you forward, based on your view. You also can hover your mouse over the smaller monthly grid on the left and scroll quickly through the months.

Add Events

You can add events to your calendar by simply clicking in the place where you need the event. If you are in the Day, Week, or 4 Days views, you can click in any half-hour space to add an event for that time; in the Month view, click on any day to automatically add an all-day event. The only exception here is the Agenda view, which does not allow you to add events by clicking in the window, although you can still add events using the other methods outlined later in this section.

When you add an event, you need to provide a name for the event. However, you often need to change other details of the event. For example, all events added in the Day, Month, and 4 Days views are assumed to be one-hour events, and all events added in the Month view are assumed to be all-day events. As the majority of things I need to track on the calendar are all-day events, I tend to stay in the Month view, but there are times when I need shorter events. If your schedule is better viewed in one of the other views, you likewise will encounter events that are more or less than one hour. You can change the timing and other details of an event by clicking the Edit event details link. This will display the event in its own page, from which you can change the tim-

TIP

You quickly can alter the starting time for an event by including the time in the name if you use the Month view. For example, in the Month view, you can create a one-hour event by entering "Dinner with Editor 6pm". The calendar will add an event called Dinner with Editor, and set it as a one-hour event beginning at 6pm. This is a really great feature that saves me a lot of time when I need to add events that are not all day. Unfortunately, it does not work on other views.

ing, along with adding details, such as the location and description of the event, configuring reminders, and changing how the calendar shows your time if you share the calendar with others.

You also can add events by clicking the Create Event button on the far-left side of the screen. This takes you directly to the event details page to add any and all information you need. The Quick Add link opens a small window into which you can type the name, time, and date of the event; the window includes an example of how to add an event. Both of these work in any view, including Agenda; in fact, they are the only ways to add events while in Agenda view.

You can edit an event's details at any time or delete the event by clicking on it in the calendar and then selecting the appropriate option.

Adding Other Calendars

Before switching to Google Calendar, I was a longtime Outlook calendar user. In

Outlook, I used to differentiate between business and personal events by color-coding, and it took me some time to figure out how to mimic this functionality in Google. As it turns out, you cannot directly color-code events; instead, you need to create individual calendars for each set of events you want to track. Although this seemed to require a lot of extra work when I first started using the calendar, I have discovered that it is, in fact, an extremely effective way to work. Separating events onto individual calendars allows you to quickly filter your calendar view to see only the events on that calendar. Also, you can share individual calendars with others, so, for example, I have several clients who have access to my work calendar so that they can know when I already am scheduled elsewhere, but they do not see my personal calendar. Likewise, I keep all school-related events for my kids on a separate calendar that I then can share easily with their grandparents.

You can add a new calendar by simply clicking the Add link in the My Calendars section on the left side of the screen. You need to give the calendar a name, but all of the other settings are optional. I have never exactly figured out where Google displays the description, so I never provide it. Users who work with people in other time zones likely will find the per-calendar time zone setting useful, while sharing the calendar will be discussed later.

Each calendar is automatically color-coded, which will determine the color of the bar indicating events on that calendar, but you can change the color by clicking on the small arrow to the right of the calendar's name after you get back to the main calendar screen. At any time, you can return to the calendar's settings page by clicking the same arrow and selecting Calendar settings.

Any event you add will be automatically added to your main or default calendar, but you can easily set an event to go onto a different calendar by choosing it in the drop-down list that will now appear when you add an event. You also can add an event to a calendar by clicking on the calendar's arrow in the left margin and selecting Create event on this calendar.

Sharing Calendars

You can share your calendars with friends, family, co-workers, clients, and anyone else you might want. Each calendar can be configured individually; again, this is one of the biggest advantages of the Google system of separating events onto individual calendars. You can share a calendar by clicking the arrow button to the right of the calendar name in the left margin of the screen and selecting Calendar Settings. Then click the Share this calendar link.

You now have two options: You can make the calendar public, allowing anyone with the proper URL to access it, or you can share it with specific people. Many organizations rely on public calendars to share event information with members. As mentioned earlier, I rely on sharing my calendars with individuals such as my wife, my parents, and select clients.

When sharing with individuals, you can enter their e-mail address and then decide what permissions they have on the calendar. You can allow them to merely view the calendar, view your time as free or busy, make changes to events, or make changes and manage permissions for others.

Adding Public Calendars

Google, along with many third parties, make public calendars available. Although you cannot edit these calendars, you can display their events in your calendar. You can add one of these calendars by clicking the Add button under the Other calendars section on the left side of the screen and selecting Browse Interesting Calendars. You can add holidays from just about any country in the world, add the schedule for your favorite sports team, or add birthdays from your contacts, moon phases, and more. After you find a calendar you like, simply click the Subscribe link.

Adding Individual Calendars

If another Google user has shared a calendar with you, you can add it to your calendar. Click the same Add link you used earlier to access public calendars, but select Add a friend's calendar. You need to add the contact's e-mail address in the box that appears. If the calendar has been shared with you, it simply is added. If not, you are given the opportunity to send an e-mail to the person asking the person to share his or her calendar.

Using Google Calendar on Your Device

Now that you understand how to use and manage the calendar on your computer, we can switch over and look at using it on your device.

Viewing the Calendar

Your device will have shipped with a Calendar application, which will be available in your Applications bin. The calendar will open in the Day view, showing today and any events you might have scheduled for today (see Figure 6.2).

Switching Views

You can switch to other views by pressing your device's Menu button, which will display options to view the calendar in the Agenda, Week, and Month views. Ironically, the designed-for-small-screens 4 Days view is not available on the very small mobile screens. The daily and weekly views display as many details of the events as they can in the space available, and the Month view simply displays bars representing events (see Figure 6.3). You can select any day on the Month view to switch back to Day view to see the details of the event.

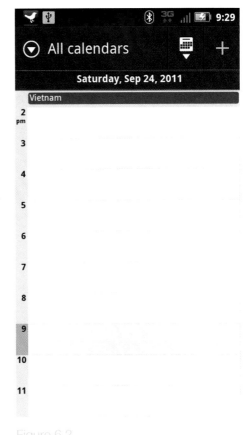

Figure 6.2

The default Day view on the Calendar

Adding Events on Your Device

You can add events on your device basically the same way you add them on the computer. In the Day and Month views, long-press at the time you want to add the event and then select New event from the menu that appears. This displays the Create event screen that allows you to add all of the same information for the event that you would have on the computer.

Viewing Calendars

Any events on any calendars you have set up on your computer will display on your

Figure 6.3

The Month view on the device

device. You can press the Menu button, then More, then View calendars to see a list of your calendars. From this screen, you can press Menu again to add another calendar, or uncheck calendars you don't want to see on your device.

Reminders

Events can have reminders associated with them to let you know when they are about to begin. When using the computer interface, reminders simply send an e-mail at the scheduled time before the event, but on your device, they display in your Notifications Bar and will play a sound—for me, at least, a much more effective reminder than simply receiving an e-mail. You can set the reminder when you create the event by pressing the device's Menu button, selecting Add reminder, and then selecting the appropriate value in the pop-up menu. You can select the X button to the left of the Reminder pop-up to remove a reminder if you do not want it. You also can add a reminder to an event by pressing the Menu button while adding an event.

Calendar Settings

You can access the calendar's settings by pressing the Menu button from any of the calendar's main views, and then selecting More and then Settings. The primary settings revolve around how reminders should work, so you can set the ringtone to play and the default reminder time. You also have the option of setting whether the Week view displays all seven days or just Monday–Friday.

Using a Calendar Home Screen Widget

Some varieties of Android may include a home screen widget for the Calendar (and can download some from the Market, too). The version that ships on the Droid X includes one that displays the current date and any events happening either today or tomorrow; I can select the widget to open the Calendar's Day view (see Figure 6.4). Other varieties of Android may include a slightly different widget.

TO-DO LIST

The Android operating system does not include a to-do list application by default. However, many to-do applications exist in the Market. One popular free application is Astrid.

When you first launch the application, you get an essentially blank screen with a text box at the bottom for you to begin entering tasks. After entering a task name, you can simply select the blue Plus sign to the left of the text box to add the task.

You also can tap the icon to the right of the task name to open a truly impressive list of options for the task. These options can be accessed for an already-existing task by long-pressing it in the task list and selecting Edit Task.

The Advanced tab of the settings enables you to configure task reminders, control its visibility, and set how often it should repeat. The Add-ons tab enables you to add the task to your calendar and track your time while working on the task.

ALARM CLOCK

I have never much cared to rely on the alarm clocks in hotel rooms, since I tend to have problems figuring out how to set them, and I am always afraid that the volume will either be too high or too low or that the radio alarm will be set to some station I

Figure 6.4

The Motorola Calendar widget

would never want to wake up to. All of those concerns are a thing of the past thanks to the alarm clock provided in my device. The Alarm application is included as part of the Android system and is available in the Applications bin.

The alarm is incredibly simple to use: Select one of the alarms to access its settings. You can name the alarm if you want, or simply set its time. You also can configure exactly which ringtone or sound you want to use, and you can even configure the alarm to play one of the MP3s or videos on your device. For those who are not inclined to wake up when the alarm goes off, there is even a backup alarm setting to play a loud beep if you ignore the main alarm.

When the alarm goes off, you can simply slide the bar to respond to it (see Figure 6.5). The settings screen enables you to configure whether sliding the bar dismisses the alarm or sets it to snooze so that it will remind you again in a few minutes.

A nice feature of the alarm is the ability to save as many alarms as you want. The application comes with three alarms set by default, but you can press the Menu button to add more, so if you have a series of important

events to which you need reminders throughout the day, you can set them all at once.

The alarm clock also can serve as a timer. By selecting the Timer tab at the top of the screen, you can set the amount of time you want to count down from and choose Start (see Figure 6.6). The timer's settings, accessible via the Menu button, enable you to change the sound that should play when the timer goes off, set the device to vibrate, and set a backup alarm.

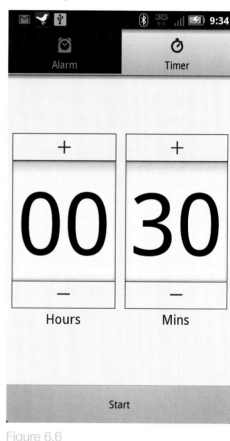

Figure 6.6

Setting the timer

Figure 6.5

The alarm

PART II

Maps, Music, Pictures, and the Web

Maps

The Skim

I have to admit to being something of a map geek. For as long as I can remember, I have loved exploring maps. In college, my roommate and I had an awesome map of Antarctica on our wall; someday, I need to ask him what happened to it. I cannot bear to hear of someplace and not have any idea where it is.

The first generation of online maps did not foster my love of cartography. Those early maps were so painfully slow that they managed to suck whatever pleasure one might have gleaned from them; certainly, simply exploring the world was not a realistic option when each page could take 30 or more seconds to load. Today, however, not only can I waste hours randomly scrolling through maps online, I can do it on my phone. As a friend of mine likes to say, living in the future sure is cool.

USING GOOGLE MAPS

Google Maps changed how many of us get directions in as big a way as Google Search changed the ways in which we find information online. Google certainly did not invent online maps, but it did figure out how to do it right, by providing an interface through which users

TIP

Watch your battery! Few things drain your device's battery faster than GPS, so whenever you have Maps or any other application that uses it running, you are reducing your battery power dramatically. Merely locking your device while Maps is up does not shut down the application nor turn off GPS, which is something I learned the hard way on my first Android phone. You need to avoid long-term use of GPS anytime you are not going to be able to plug in your device either while you use it or shortly after.

Figure 7.1

Maps, showing my location (blue arrow) by default

could easily scroll around on the map and zoom in and out, and most important, it made sure that it would all be fast. Later, Google added services that made Maps even cooler, with things like satellite imagery and traffic reports.

Although finding directions from home works, being able to take those directions with you without having to waste paper is even better, and, of course, Google integrated its Maps application into Android from the very beginning.

You can open Maps from the Applications bin, but it is one of those applications that you are almost certainly going to want to add to your home screen as a shortcut. When you first open Maps, it should open to your current location, thanks to your device's GPS system (see Figure 7.1).

When viewing a map, you can zoom in and out using the buttons in the lower-right corner of the screen. You can also zoom in and out by pinching the screen — place two

fingers relatively far from each other and bring them closer while remaining in contact with the screen to zoom out, or use the opposite action to zoom in.

SEARCH IN MAPS

Most of the time, when you use the web-based interface for Google Maps, you begin by searching for an address. You can do the same in Maps on your phone — simply type the location into the search box at the top of the screen. You also can select the microphone button and speak your destination;

this is a particularly useful, not to mention safe, feature for using Maps while driving. Assuming that the address you searched for was found, its location will now display on the map. If more than one possible location is found, Maps will display a list of results.

GETTING DIRECTIONS

After you find a location on Maps, you can get directions to that location. When your search location appears, select the balloon tip that is displaying the address to see a screen with additional options for that location. Select Directions, and you will be shown a screen where you can confirm the starting and ending locations, and then choose between Navigate and Get directions. See the next section for details on Navigate; for now, select Get directions to have the map generate driving directions.

The app will now highlight your route and display the first step in the directions. Arrows at the bottom of the Map view enable you to step through the directions, while the small square icon in the bottom-left corner displays the directions list view.

GETTING THERE WITHOUT A CAR

If you would prefer to get where you need by foot, bicycle, or bus, Maps can help. When you look up an address and choose to get directions, you see four buttons along the top of the screen, just under the addresses. The first, a picture of a car, is the one that is selected by default and gives you driving directions. The second button with the bus picture gives you directions via public transit. The transit directions use any form of public transit available in

TIP

Whether searching on your device or on the web, you do not need to know a specific address in order to find a location in Google Maps. You can search for an intersection by typing the names of the streets, so, for example, you could search for "Pennsylvania Ave and Executive Ave, Washington, DC" to find the corner near the White House. You also can search for local businesses near an address or landmark, so searching for "hotels near San Diego convention center" will give you ideas of where to stay for next year's Comic-Con. One of the coolest tips, though, will likely work only on your device: searching "pizza near me" will show all of the pizza restaurants near your current location.

your area, including bus, train, subway, and ferry. The directions show options based on your time of departure (see Figure 7.2), and the system creates a route that takes into account necessary transfers. A particularly nice feature is the included indicators for the fares each leg of the trip will require.

Bicycle and walking directions (with appropriate icons) take into account the differences afforded by those choices. Bike routes take into account special bike trails, and in big cities, they stick as much as possible to routes with dedicated bike lanes and avoid rider-unfriendly parts of the route like big hills. Walking directions ignore things like one-way roads and, similar to bike routes, keep you on as flat a route as possible and stick to walking trails if possible.

THROW AWAY YOUR GPS DEVICE

In early 2010, Google rolled out a new, free application to many Android users, Navigate, which provides audio turn-by-turn navigation to your destination. Given that I frequently travel to new cities, I had at times considered purchasing a dedicated GPS device, but I am very glad I waited. Why would I need a special device, along with its monthly subscription fees, when my phone does it for me?

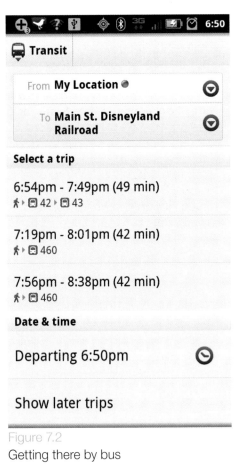

Figure 7.2

Getting there by bus

Whenever you search for an address and then ask for directions in Maps, it will ask whether you want to use Maps (Get directions) or Navigate. Navigate generally takes a few seconds to load, but after it does, you will see your route highlighted on the screen. The orientation switches to that roughly first-person perspective you probably have seen in dedicated GPS navigation systems (see Figure 7.3). You then receive turn-by-turn directions as you drive, using Navigate's built-in text-to-speech voice, which my daughter decided was named Sierra.

When you reach your destination, you should turn Navigate off. If it keeps running, even in the background, it will drain your battery very quickly. Press the Menu button on your phone and choose Exit Navigate to close it and save battery life.

By the way, I was kidding in the heading about throwing away your GPS device. Like all modern electronics, it has all kinds of nasty chemicals in it, so be sure to recycle it instead!

VIEW LIVE TRAFFIC

Maps will show you live traffic reports, allowing you to route yourself around problem areas. You can turn this feature on by pressing the Menu button on your phone and then selecting Layers. Select Traffic, and the map updates to display traffic reports. Green lines on roads mean that everything is fine; yellow lines mean you should expect traffic to be slow but still moving, and red roads are the ones you want to avoid (see Figure 7.4). Road hazards are displayed as well: An orange triangle icon signifies construction, while an icon of a collision signifies some other hazard, such as an accident or disabled vehicle.

Figure 7.3
Turn-by-turn directions, thanks to Navigate

TIDBIT

Google collects traffic data from a variety of sources, but one of them is reading this book right now. Your GPS-enabled phone actually transmits your location and speed to Google in real time. Although I had long suspected this was the case, I actually confirmed it for myself one evening when I was driving along a rural road. Maps showed the route as green, which it was because I was the only car for miles. However, at one point I got hungry and pulled into a McDonald's drive-thru. As I was waiting for my food, I noticed that the road I had been on, which was still deserted, now was showing red, because the only data Google had at that moment was coming from a car that was stopped. By the way, if this triggers any lingering *1984* fears you might have, you can choose to opt out of the My Location system on your phone. Details on how to do this can be found at www.google.com/support/mobile.

OTHER LAYERS

The Layers feature in Google Maps allows you to see the world in a variety of different ways. Traffic is a layer, but others exist as well. Each of these layers can be accessed by pressing your phone's Menu button, and then selecting Layers.

Satellite Photos

Instead of the traditional drawn map, you can view your route using satellite images. Personally, I tend to prefer the map view

when I need to travel, but I have found the satellite view useful on occasion when trying to find a location: Seeing what the area around my destination actually looks like can be very helpful when I get close.

Terrain Maps

Another layer available on Google Maps is Terrain. Hikers would find this particularly useful in planning routes.

Figure 7.4

Monday afternoon traffic in New York City — Yuck!

Latitude

Google Latitude enables you to share your location with others and easily connect when nearby. When you select the Latitude layer, it displays your current location. You can select your name to display a list of options, including Send location to others. You have the option to broadcast this location on Facebook, Twitter, or other social networks, as well as text or e-mail it. If you join Latitude through its dedicated app, you also can send and receive invitations from friends and then easily dis-

cover their location. More information on Latitude is available at www.google.com/mobile.

Recent Places

The final set of options on the Layers menu lists the locations you have most recently searched, making it easy to look up a recent location and display it on the map.

More Layers

Select the More Layers button at the bottom of the Layers menu screen to see additional choices. The My Maps option displays maps you have created and saved on the Google Maps Web page. More details on creating and saving maps can be found at http://maps.google.com/support. The Bicycling layer displays local bike paths and routes (see Figure 7.5), and Wikipedia overlays icons on the map that link to Wikipedia entries for your area. The Transit Lines layer displays bus, train, and subway maps (see Figure 7.6). Finally, Favorite Places enables you to view maps created by other users.

DRIVING WITH YOUR PHONE

Features like Navigate are obviously most useful when used in your car. They are less useful, however, if your phone is simply sitting on the center console or in your pocket; in order to really benefit from the turn-by-turn directions, you need to be able to see your phone. You can maximize both the safety and convenience of these features by purchasing a car dock, which is a device designed to securely hold your phone on your dashboard. Each model of phone has

Figure 7.5

Bike paths in Sacramento, California

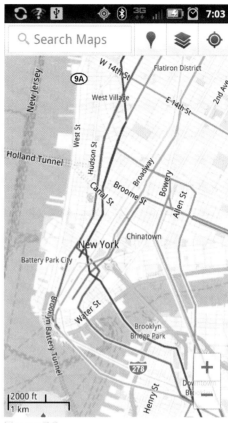

Figure 7.6

New York City's transit map

a car dock specifically designed for it, so be sure to get the right one. Most car docks include a car charger, so if you are planning on getting a dock, you may not need to spend the additional money on a separate charger.

Many newer Android phones include a CarDock application that puts the phone into a state ready to use in your car. The phone automatically should detect when it has been put in the dock and switch to car mode by itself; if it does not, you can launch the application manually. The application includes six oversized, easy-

to-hit buttons. Five are preprogrammed for music, maps, calling, voice search, and closing the application. The sixth is customizable and can be linked to any other application on your phone. When I first began playing with CarDock, I set this sixth button to the camera, which seemed kind of fun. When I was done playing, though, I reset it to launch the application I use the most in the car: TuneInRadio, which allows me to listen to Internet radio stations.

Whenever I drive, I keep the phone in the dock. I usually launch TuneInRadio and set

TIDBIT

GPS stands for Global Positioning System. Although consumer-level GPS is relatively new, the technology has been around for a while. The U.S. government began work on it in 1973, with the system becoming fully operational by 1995. The system relies on between 24 and 32 satellites and is still funded by the U.S. government and run by the U.S. Air Force. The system was designed to allow the Air Force and Navy to more precisely locate and control military assets, but following the 1983 destruction of Korean Air Lines flight 007, which was shot down after straying accidentally into restricted Soviet airspace, the U.S. government opened the system to civilian use as well. Today's GPS is capable of providing a location anywhere on the planet to within 20 meters, or about 65 feet.

it to the station I want to listen to, and then select the My Location button in CarDock. This ties directly into Google Maps, so if you have a layer already turned on, it will display; I almost always leave Traffic on. CarDock includes a few additional features, such as a speed and direction indicator in the bottom-left corner of the map. You can also search for a location and turn on Navigate to have your docked phone look and act just like a dedicated GPS device.

When you receive a call while the phone is docked, it will interrupt whatever else the application may be doing to display the incoming call. If you have a Bluetooth headset or other hands-free device, you can accept the call by simply selecting the

appropriate button , or possibly just saying "Answer". If you do not have a hands-free device, you can still accept the call, at which point CarDock will turn on the speaker phone, in theory allowing you to have your conversation without needing to hold the phone to your ear. I say "theoretically" because although it does work, you will find that the noise in your car will likely be too loud to really talk on the phone this way.

A particularly nice feature of the dock is the integrated jack on the back that allows you to plug your phone in, because many features — particularly Navigate — would otherwise quickly drain the battery. Be aware, however, that your phone is likely sitting exposed on your dashboard and is susceptible to overheating, something that has happened to me on several occasions when it has been more than 100 degrees outside. When the phone begins to overheat, the first thing it will do is stop charging, so you should glance at the Notifications Bar every now and then and note whether you are still charging. If it occurs, remove the phone from the dock and move it someplace out of the sun until it can cool down. It is also possible that given that you are using the screen, GPS, Navigate, and other applications, the car charger will not be able to actually charge the phone, but will instead just keep it from discharging. Thus, you may find that when you arrive at your destination, your battery will not be at 100 percent.

Many newer cars include an input jack to allow you to plug a device into the car stereo. Because your phone uses a standard jack for the headphone, you can plug your phone in and listen to music, Internet radio, or Navigate's directions over the car's speakers.

STREET VIEW

Street view is perhaps one of Google's best-known features of Maps, so it is fairly surprising that although it is available on your phone, it is very well hidden. Street view allows you to see photographs of an area on the map, complete with 360-degree views. If you need to find a business or something in an unfamiliar location, this can allow you to see the area to which you are traveling. Note that like satellite photos, Street view is not live.

To access Street view, you need to zoom in on the map. As you get close to the ground, you begin to see buildings rendered in 3-D. At this point, you can long-press on a point on the map, which displays an address. Select the address to bring up a screen with details of that address, and you should see an icon on the far right of a person with an arrow. If the icon is grayed out, you have not zoomed in far enough to use Street view.

If you have zoomed in enough, the icon will be active, and selecting it will display that location in Street view (see Figure 7.7). You can swipe your finger to turn the view around and see around you, or use the dark arrows to move forward or backward.

GOOGLE PLACES

Recent versions of Google Maps include a new feature called Google Places, which displays information on restaurants, coffee shops, bars, hotels, attractions, ATMs, and gas stations near your current location. Places can be accessed by selecting the pushpin icon at the top of the Google Maps

Figure 7.7

Google Headquarters in Mountain View, California, as seen on Street view

screen. Selecting this icon displays a menu of categories; selecting a category from this menu displays businesses matching that category. You then can select any of these locations to bring up more details about a business, get directions to it, or call the business directly.

INSTALL A COMPASS

Your phone includes an internal compass that, among other things, ensures that the Navigate arrow is pointing in the right direction. The Android Market includes

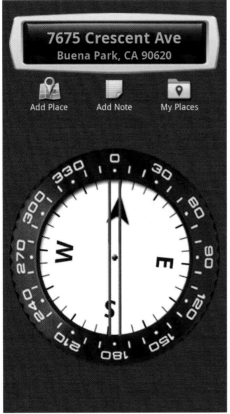

7675 Crescent Ave
Buena Park, CA 90620

Add Place   Add Note   My Places

Figure 7.8

The Compass application

a Compass application that displays this directional awareness as a traditional compass (see Figure 7.8).

When you first launch the compass, it will prompt you to calibrate it by waving the phone in a figure-8 pattern several times. You might want to do this when no one else is around because you will look rather silly doing it.

You can press the Menu button to change the settings of the compass, including changing the type to look like an antique compass or a GPS device that includes your speed, pitch, and roll.

FIND OUT WHERE YOU WERE WITH MY TRACKS

The My Tracks application, available in the Market, enables you to track your location while walking, hiking, or other activities. These recorded paths then can be uploaded and saved and shared either as custom Google Maps or Google Docs. You can also view live statistics of your path while you go.

The first time you launch My Tracks, you need to agree to the license agreement and then, if you want, read the provided help file. After that, you are taken to a map that displays your current location. You can press the Menu button on your phone and select Record Track to begin recording. Then simply walk, run, hike, or drive the path you want to take. While on your route, you can select the map and then select the right arrow button that appears to view a screen of statistics about your track, or the left arrow to view an elevation profile.

When you have completed your path or route, you can again press the Menu button and then select Stop Recording, which displays a Track Details page, where you can give the track a name, input the type of activity, and describe the track. When complete, select Save.

To share the track, select the plus icon in the bottom-right corner of the screen and select the option you want to use. The Send to Google option uploads the map to either Google Maps or Google Docs, and Share with Friends enables you to e-mail a link to the map or send the track in one of several file formats.

USE GOOGLE EARTH

Few applications have brought out the map geek in me more than Google Earth.

Earth is an amazing application that combines Google's database of satellite imagery together in a single, easy-to-explore interface. Earth was developed by another company, Keyhole, and released under its current Google Earth name in 2005. It now can be downloaded for free from the Android Market, bringing all of its coolness to your device.

When you first launch Google Earth, you can pretend momentarily that you are an astronaut, as you will see Earth from a distance that so far has only been viewed by the Apollo astronauts.

You can rotate the globe by simply sliding your finger over it, and zoom in by either moving two fingers apart from one another on the screen or by double-tapping. Eventually, details begin to appear. When you are in far enough to make out details, you will see yellow squares marking designated locations; selecting any of these will bring up a screen detailing that location. You can press your device's Back button to return to the main Google Earth screen from these detail pages.

Normally, dragging your finger on the screen moves you around the map. You can select the Look Around icon in the bottom-left corner of the screen to change this behavior. With Look Around enabled, dragging your finger will rotate your view 360 degrees around the center of the screen. You can select the icon again to turn off Look Around, and select the compass in the top-right corner of the screen to return to a north-is-up orientation.

With Look Around turned on, you can tilt your view so that rather than looking from above, you can see the world from more of an angle. You can tilt down by dragging upward on the screen (see Figure 7.9), or tilt up by dragging down on the screen. Although the directions may seem backward — you drag up to tilt down, and drag down to tilt up — they actually make a lot of sense when you are interacting with the application.

No Google application would be complete without Search, and Google Earth is no different. Press the Menu button on your phone and select Search, or press your phone's Search button. Then type what you are looking for, whether it is an address, landmark, business, or just about anything else. For the most part, the same searches that work on Google Maps work here. The main difference is the cool factor: In Maps, you are simply taken to your destination, while in Earth, you get to fly there. When the original Google Earth application was released, one reviewer described the animation as an "ICBM view," which is apt as it will look like you take off, fly over the planet, and then dive in on your location (see Figure 7.10).

Unfortunately, many of the desktop application's really neat features are missing in this first version of the Android application, including the ability to go back in time and see older satellite photos of regions (using this ability to see pictures of New Orleans before and after Katrina is particularly moving) and exploring the Moon and Mars. Hopefully, Google will add them as time goes by.

Figure 7.9

Seeing Sacramento at an angle

Figure 7.10

"ICBM view" of Google Earth

Music

The Skim

M y entire music collection exists today as MP3s. We have a really cool CD rack we bought from Ikea on the wall of our living room, but honestly it exists mostly for decoration. On the rare occasion that I still purchase a CD, I bring it home and immediately rip it or convert it to MP3s on the computer. The CD itself finds its way to the Ikea case, never to be seen or heard again. I know I am not alone here, either; I cannot think of anyone I know who still uses actual CDs as their primary source for music, and why would they? Why would I want to listen to a single album, and have to keep interrupting myself to change albums, when I can create a playlist of all of the songs I want to listen to and just let it play? This is even more true when you consider that today you can bring your music collection with you anywhere you go. Best of all, you do not need to buy and carry around a separate MP3 player, either.

PREPARING MUSIC FOR YOUR PHONE

In order to transfer music from a CD to your phone, you first need to convert it to the correct format. Dozens of programs exist that are capable of performing this task, but the most popular is Apple's iTunes application. If you own a Mac, you already have iTunes installed; if you use Windows, you can download it free from www.apple.com.

Ripping CDs

You can transfer the music from a CD to your computer's hard drive via a process known as ripping the CD. To do this, simply insert the CD into your computer's drive with iTunes running. The program will detect the CD and ask whether you want to import it into your iTunes library (see Figure 8.1). Click Yes, and the program begins ripping the songs from the CD.

When the ripping process is complete, you can click Music from the Library menu on the left side of the screen to see the songs that

have been downloaded (see Figure 8.2). Unlike many programs, iTunes does not directly display the location of the music on your hard drive, as it assumes that you will use the program to perform all tasks on the songs. However, if you are curious as to where exactly the music is stored, you can right-click on a track and select Get Info. The file's location is displayed at the bottom of the dialog box.

Change iTunes Settings

iTunes automatically converts your tracks to M4A format. This format should be fully supported by your Android device and practically any other media player you want to use, but if you need or want to use the more common MP3 format, you can change the

Figure 8.1

iTunes asking whether I want to import a CD onto my machine

Figure 8.2
The CD's tracks, now transferred to my computer, displaying in the iTunes library

settings in iTunes to accommodate that. Click Edit and then Preferences. On the first tab of the Preferences dialog box, select Import Settings. In the Import Settings dialog box, change the Import Using drop-down from the default AAC Encoder to MP3 Encoder. The Preferences dialog box also can be used to change the default location to which iTunes copies music files by clicking the Advanced tab, and then Change.

Download Album Art

iTunes can download album art for your albums, which displays both in the iTunes library when you listen to the album on your computer as well as on your device. In order to download album art, however, you first need to create an account with iTunes and log into the iTunes Store. You can do this directly within iTunes by clicking the iTunes Store link on the menu at the left. Then click Sign In in the top-right corner. If you already have an account, you can enter your username and password; if you do not have an account yet, click Create New Account (see Figure 8.3).

After you are logged in, you can return to your music library. Then right-click the album and select Get Album Artwork. You need to confirm that, yes, you really did want to download the artwork — I would suggest that you select the Do not ask me again option on this useless dialog box — and the album art will appear.

TIP

No discussion of working with music files would be complete without a discussion of copyright issues. When you purchase an audio CD, you have the legal right to copy that music to another medium such as your computer so long as you are going to use that music only for you to listen to. You cannot distribute the music files to others or use it for any public performance. You can find many more details on this and other issue surrounding copyright from the U.S. Copyright Office's Web site at www.copyright.gov/.

DOWNLOADING MUSIC TO YOUR DEVICE

iTunes does not support directly synching songs between itself and non-Apple devices, but you can still transfer music between your computer and device manually. Although some other media players on your computer may support directly transferring songs, the steps outlined in this chapter work regardless of the software you use.

To transfer your music, you first need to plug your device into your computer's USB port and mount your SD card. You can mount your card by pulling down the Notifications Bar and selecting USB connection. Then depending on your version of Android, select either Mount card or PC

Figure 8.3

Log into iTunes using an existing account or create a new one.

Mode or USB Mass Storage. See Chapter 1 for a discussion on the differences between PC Mode and USB Mass Storage.

When mounted, your device's SD card should appear as a drive on your computer. More and more phones now have internal storage that also shows as a drive when connected. So with a lot of phones, you'll actually see TWO drives. From here, you can drag-and-drop music files from whatever folder iTunes stored them in to the Music folder on your device.

PURCHASING MUSIC VIA AMAZON MP3

In addition to copying music from your computer to your device, you also can purchase music directly on your device. Although many applications exist to do this, most Android devices come with a preinstalled application to enable you to purchase music from Amazon. You can launch the Amazon MP3 app from your Application Launcher. From here, you can either search for a song or album or browse bestselling albums, songs, or genres (see Figure 8.4). When you find what you are looking for, you can select the album to display the tracks. From here, you can either purchase the entire album or individual songs by selecting the price and then selecting it again when it turns into a Buy button.

Next, you are prompted to log into your Amazon.com account; you can click the link at the top of the dialog box to create one if necessary. As soon as you log in, the purchase process begins automatically and cannot be cancelled, so be sure you want to purchase the album before entering your username and password.

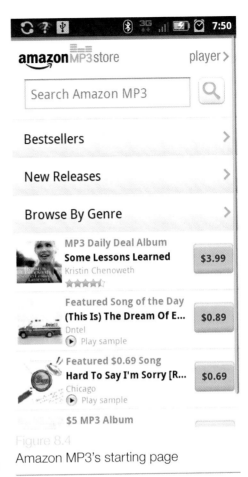

Figure 8.4

Amazon MP3's starting page

Note that the Amazon MP3 store is not available in some countries, so it is possible that your device will not support it, depending on your location.

LISTENING TO MUSIC

After you have your music on your device, you can use Android's built-in music player to listen to it. Simply launch the Music app from your Application Launcher to see a list of the albums on your device (see Figure 8.5). Choose an album to see a list of the tracks, and select any song to begin playing.

109

While a song is playing, you can pause it or move to the previous or next song using the buttons at the bottom of the screen. You also can drag the slider to move backward or forward through a song or press and hold your finger on the Forward or Back buttons to fast-forward or fast-reverse the current song. Higher on the screen, just below the album art, are three buttons that enable you to return to the track list, shuffle the songs to play the album in a random order, or repeat the current song. You also can select the album art itself to switch between the art and an animated visualization while the

song plays. You can use your device's Back button to return to the track list and then use the button again to return to the album list. From here, you can view your music by artist or song. You can also select the Play-lists tab to display any playlists you may have on your device; see "Creating Playlists" later in this chapter.

You can use any other function of your device while a song is playing. Simply press the Home button to return to the home screen. The Notifications Bar displays an icon letting you know that a song is playing; you can pull the Notifications Bar down to view the title, album, and artist of the song. Select the notification to return to the Now Playing screen.

Your music also continues playing when the device sleeps. On some versions of Android, the Lock screen displays the current song and provides buttons that enable you to pause, skip forward, and skip back without unlocking your device (see Figure 8.6).

CREATING PLAYLISTS

Often, you want to play songs from more than one album. You might have a mix of songs you happen to like, or perhaps have a series of albums you listen to in succession. Either of these can be handled easily with a playlist. You can create playlists from songs currently on your device. To do this, long-press a song — either directly in the Library's Song list or in an album list — and select Add to playlist (see Figure 8.7). Select New and type a name for the playlist. You can then add additional songs to the playlist by long-pressing the song, choosing Add to playlist, and then selecting your playlist.

Figure 8.5
The album list in the Music app

You can delete playlists you no longer need by long-pressing them in the Playlists section of the Library and selecting Delete. Note that deleting a playlist does not delete the list's songs from your device.

GOOGLE MUSIC

In mid-2011, Google joined Apple, Amazon, and other technologies companies in providing an online streaming music service, technically called Music Beta by Google, but referred to by pretty much everyone as Google Music. A few things

differentiate Google Music from its competitors. First, it is, at least as of this writing, free for up to 20,000 songs. And second, because it is from Google, it enjoys a close association with Android.

Signing Up and Uploading Your Collection

To use Google Music, you need to sign up for the beta. To do this, you must visit http://music.google.com and use your Google account to request an invitation. If you know someone who is already using

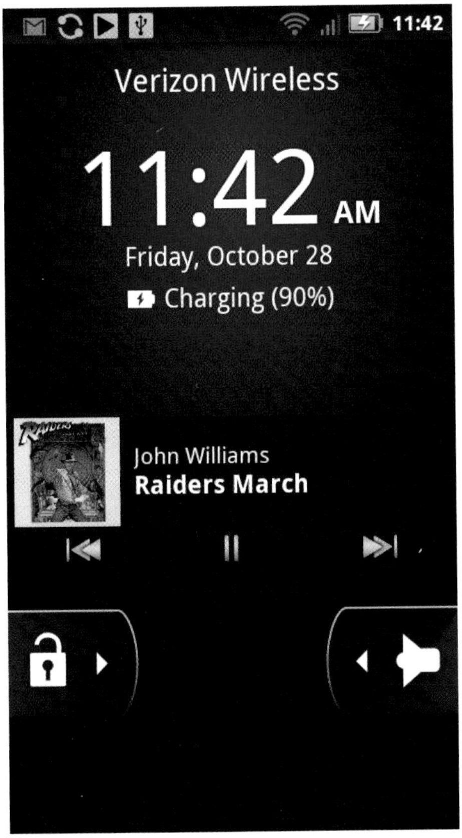

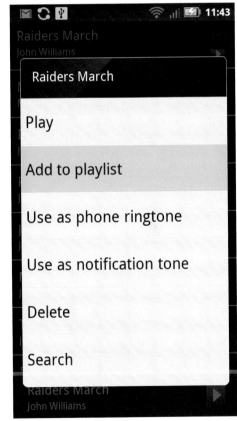

Figure 8.6
The Lock screen showing the current song; not available on all devices

Figure 8.7
Long-press a song to display the menu with the Add to playlist option.

ALTERNATE APP

Many other applications exist for managing and listening to music on your phone. Two particularly popular apps are TuneWiki and Meridian Player. TuneWiki, which is available in a free, ad-supported version or for purchase for $4.99 without ads, enables you to both play songs on your phone as well as stream tunes from Internet radio stations. The free Meridian Player includes features similar to TuneWiki's, minus the Internet radio. Both are available on the Android Market.

Google Music, that person can send you an invitation as well. As of now, invitations are only being made available to those in the United States, but the company has said that it plans to make the service more widely available later.

Once you receive your invitation in your inbox, you can return to the website and get started. The first thing you will need to do is upload your collection to the service, which is quite easy thanks to the free Music Manager application that can be downloaded from the site and is available for both Windows and Macintosh. Enter your Google username and password into the application, then point it at the folder or folders in which your music is stored to begin uploading. Then wait. It took the service the better part of a weekend to upload my collection, currently at just under 10,000 songs. A nice feature of the service is that it will continually monitor your selected folder or folders, so as you add new music, it will be automatically uploaded.

Once you have your music online, you can listen to it from just about anywhere by simply visiting music.google.com again. All of your albums will display (see Figure 8.8). Simply select the album you want to hear and click the Play button at the bottom of your screen.

Listening On Your Device

You can also listen to any songs you have uploaded to Google Music on your Android device. First, you need the new Music player, available from the Market. While the app's name is simply Music, a search on that term alone is likely to return too many results, so searching for "Google Music" will likely be more successful. You are looking for the app with the set of headphones as its icon.

Download the app and it will automatically sync with the Google account associated with your device. Herein lies one issue with the Google Music service: The service can only be associated with a single Google account, as can your device. This means that there is no way for me to set up my wife's phone to use my Google Music account. In order for us both to be able to listen to our music, we had to create a second Google Music account for her, and then upload all of our songs to her account. It is a hassle, to say the least, and a shortcoming that I hope Google fixes eventually. It seems that allowing the app to be logged in as a different user than the device would be an easy fix, if anyone from Google happens to be reading this.

Once you have the app installed, all of your songs will appear (see Figure 8.9). At this point, you can use the Music app just as you would the built-in music player: Simply find the song you want to listen to and press play. Be aware, however, that the app needs to download at least a portion of the song before it can play, so there will be a slight delay when you first listen to a song.

Listening Offline

Google Music is a great way to have your entire music collection with you at all times, but it relies on a Wi-Fi or data connection. If you are some place where you need to be offline, such as on a plane, and still want your music, you can designate certain albums, artists, and playlists to be available offline. These songs will be downloaded to your device so that you can listen to them anywhere. To do this, select the small arrow just below and to the right of the artist, album, or playlist name and select Available offline (see Figure 8.10).

ADDING A HOME SCREEN WIDGET FOR MUSIC

You can directly access your music and play songs from your home screen by adding a widget. As with other widgets, you can long-press on the home screen, select Widgets or Android Widgets, and then scroll to Music.

The widget displays the song currently playing, as well as enables you to pause the song and skip to the next song in the album or playlist (see Figure 8.11). You can also select the song directly to access the Music app.

USING SONGS AS RINGTONES AND NOTIFICATION SOUNDS

You can use a song in your library as the ringtone for your phone or for specific contacts. You can also set songs as notifi-

TIP

Another method of setting notifications and ringtones is to save your songs into a proper folder on your phone. If you connect your phone to your computer and mount it as a USB drive, you can explore its folders. You see a Music folder, which contains the songs and albums you have uploaded or synched to the phone. You also see a media folder, which contains an audio folder that, in turn, contains ringtones and notifications folders. The music player sees the songs in the Music folder, and ringtones and notifications see songs in the media folder. This is why your music player's library is not cluttered with all of the phone's ringtones, but is also why those songs do not appear when you try to set your ringtone or notification. You can copy a song into either the ringtones or notifications folder to have it appear when you set either sound on your phone.

cations for operating system events and for some applications. You can set the ringtone to a song by long-pressing the song in the library and selecting Use as phone ringtone.

You can also use songs as ringtones for specific contacts so that you can tell when they are calling without looking at your phone. Unfortunately, Android by default does not make this process obvious, as the settings for contact ringtones display only the default system tones and the phone's current ringtone. However, this actually provides a workaround. You

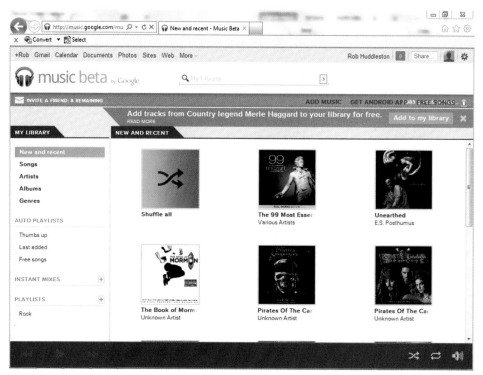

Figure 8.8

My music collection online via Google Music

need to first set the song you want to use for your contact as the phone's ringtone by following the steps outlined in the previous section. Then you can open your Contact app, select the contact you want to use, and then press the Menu button and select Edit. Scroll through the contact's details until you see the setting for Ringtone — you may need to select the Additional info bar to see it. Select the Ringtone setting, and you see the song you just set as the phone's ringtone in the list. Select it and then tap OK. Obviously, you then need to go back and reset your phone's ringtone.

Although a built-in method to make this easier would be nice, several third-party apps have been developed to solve this problem. One of the more popular is Ringdroid, which is available free in the Market. When you launch Ringdroid, it automatically brings up a list of all of the songs on your phone and includes a handy search to quickly locate a particular song. Ringdroid's primary purpose is to enable you to edit songs to use as ringtones and notifications, so when you select a song in the application, it opens the song in a new screen that shows the waveform for the song with simple buttons you can drag to set the beginning and ending points (see Figure 8.12). After you finish editing, press the phone's Menu button and select Save, at which point you are presented with a dialog box that enables you to name your edited

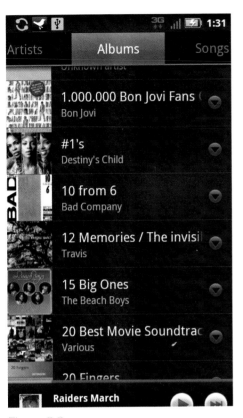

from the Market. Pandora enables you to specify artists or genres that you like, and it then plays songs not only from what you specified but from similar artists as well, enabling you to discover songs you might not otherwise know of. When you first install the app, you need to create a new free account with Pandora if you do not already have one.

Once registered, the application asks you for your favorite artist, song, or composer. It then creates a new radio station for you with songs from that artist or composer, as well as similar songs (see Figure 8.13). While a song is playing, you can select the thumbs-up or thumbs-down icons at the bottom of the screen to tell Pandora whether you like the song. If you vote thumbs down, the song immediately stops and does not play in your station again, but if you vote yes, the current song is used as criteria for picking other songs.

You can press the Menu button on your device and then the first of the icons on the

Figure 8.9
The Music app in Gingerbread, showing my entire music collection online

clip and select whether the song will be saved as a ringtone, a notification sound, alarm, or music. If you choose to save as a ringtone, you then are presented with options to set the ringtone as the default tone for your phone or assign it to a particular contact.

LISTENING TO INTERNET RADIO

Internet radio stations enable you to listen to a variety of songs, just as you would on a traditional over-the-air radio station. One of the more popular applications to listen to Internet radio is Pandora, available for free

TIDBIT

Pandora limits the number of times you can skip a song, regardless of whether you skip by giving the song a thumbs down or just use the skip button. You can skip up to six songs per hour, and if you remain with a free account, you can only skip 12 times per day. A Pandora One account, currently priced at $36 per year, lifts the daily (but not the hourly) limit, along with removing the advertising. You can get more details on subscribing at http://blog.pandora.com/faq//contents/64.html.

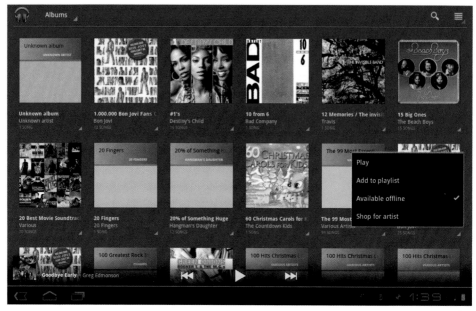

Figure 8.10
Designating an album for offline play. While the figure shows Honeycomb, the procedure is the same for older, phone-based versions of Android.

menu to display a list of your stations. From here, you can again press the Menu button and select Create Station to specify an artist or song.

IDENTIFYING MUSIC WITH SHAZAM

Science fiction author Arthur C. Clarke once stated that any sufficiently advanced technology was indistinguishable from magic. Shazam seems to prove him right. With this simply, well, magical application, you can have your device listen to any music playing, whether on the radio or over the speakers in a store or restaurant, and it will identify the song, displaying the song title and artist and even allowing you to purchase the album.

Shazam is technically a free application, meaning that you can download it without

TIDBIT

Obviously, Shazam does not actually rely on magic. Rather, it records a sample of the song it hears and submits it to Shazam's servers. There, the recording is analyzed for its "acoustic fingerprint;" that is, it looks for the song's frequency peaks and then compares it to those songs in its database. Although I have encountered many times when it was unable to find a match, I have yet to encounter a time when it gets something wrong.

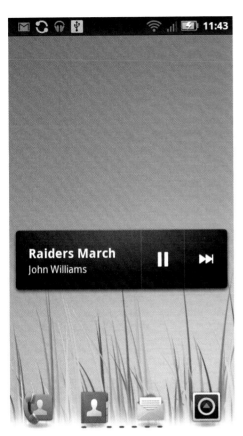

Figure 8.11
The Music home screen widget

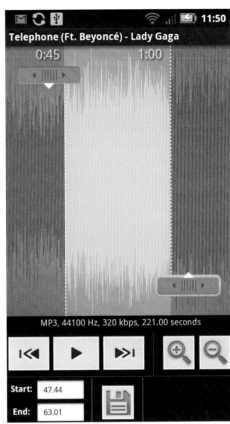

Figure 8.12
Editing a song

paying. However, the application limits free users to identifying five songs per month. If you think you need to identify more than that, you can purchase a subscription to the service.

After the application is downloaded and installed, the application could not be simpler to use. All you need to do is launch the application and select anywhere on the screen. The app takes a minute or so to listen to the music before displaying the information about the song (see Figure 8.14).

You should note that Shazam will not be able to identify absolutely every song you

try. You often cannot use it in very loud situations such as bars, as too much other noise can interfere with its ability to listen to the song. Also, it cannot identify live recordings or performances, and I have noted that it generally has trouble with classical music. Still, despite these limitations, the app is pretty darned amazing. One other word of caution: If you have kids, you might not want to let them know you have Shazam. I made the mistake of showing it to my daughter, so now when we're driving somewhere she'll often ask what song is playing. If I say I don't know,

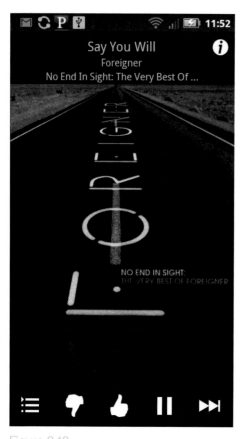

Figure 8.13

My Pandora station, based on Foreigner

Figure 8.14

A song identified by Shazam

she says, in a tone that only a nine-year-old can manage, "Dad, just get out your phone and look it up!"

DOWNLOADING AND LISTENING TO PODCASTS

A podcast is a nonstreamed audio broadcast, which is the fancy way of saying that it is a recording you can download and listen to at your leisure. The term podcast replaced the original name, webcast, thanks to the rise in people who chose to listen to them on their iPods. Many traditional radio programs are now recorded and distributed

via podcast, but a large number of podcasts today are recorded specifically for that medium.

The accepted standard for recorded podcasts is to save them as MP3s, and you can treat them as such: You can simply download the MP3, transfer it to your device, and listen to it using your device's Music player. However, most podcasts are not one-time events; rather, podcasts usually are recorded on some schedule. What really distinguishes a podcast from any other MP3 is that you can subscribe to a podcast and have them downloaded automatically as new recordings become available. Many podcasts are distributed completely free of charge, and others may require a subscription fee.

Find and Subscribe to a Podcast with Google Listen

In order to subscribe to a podcast and take advantage of automatic downloading, you need to install a podcast application such as Google Listen, available as usual from the Market. After you have the app installed, you can begin to subscribe to podcasts. Within Listen, you can search for podcasts using the search icon at the top of the screen. After you find the podcast you are looking for, select one of its episodes and then select Subscribe (see Figure 8.15).

You can listen to the current episode immediately. You also can return to the main Listen screen by pressing your device's Back button several times, and then select the My listen items link. This selection displays a list of items you have listened to or are waiting to listen to; select the title of an episode to listen.

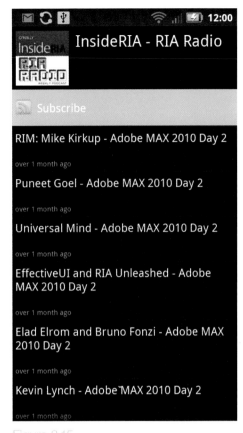

Figure 8.15
Subscribing to a podcast

Taking Pictures

The Skim

The most-photographed person in the world in the nineteenth century was Gen. George Armstrong Custer. There are around 200 known pictures of him. Even a few decades ago, taking pictures was a costly enterprise. When I visited the Soviet Union on a high school class trip, I took around 300 pictures over the course of two weeks. But that, of course, has changed, quite dramatically, in the last few years: On a recent weekend trip to Disneyland, I took close to 1,000 pictures. This meteoric rise in picture taking can be directly attributed to two factors. First, the fact that digital photography has made individual pictures free. My limit of 300 pictures on the trip to Russia was due primarily to the amount of film I could afford, but to my kids, the very concept of "film" is as outdated as a sundial. Second, and just as important, is the sudden proliferation of cameras. Today, nearly everyone owns a camera simply because nearly everyone owns a mobile device, and they are one in the same. Good news here: Although early mobile devices included cameras that took less-than-stellar pictures, today's devices contain cameras that rival what you would expect to pay several hundred dollars for in a dedicated camera.

TIDBIT

As good as the cameras included in today's devices are, they are still in the end point-and-shoot cameras. Most will not allow you to adjust things like f-stop and ISO speeds. (If you do not know what an f-stop is, then you probably don't care that your device will not allow you to change it, so you need not worry. In fact, you can go ahead and stop reading this sidebar and return to the main text.) Many cameras suffer from slow shutter speeds as well — my old G1 had such a ridiculously slow shutter that it was all but impossible to get a clear shot of anything that was not absolutely still, which is a nice way of saying that it was basically worthless for getting shots of the kids. Only the newest models even include a flash. Although it is certainly nice that your device includes a camera, keep in mind that it is still first and foremost a device. If you are really into photography, your device is not likely to replace your dSLR anytime soon.

USING YOUR DEVICE'S CAMERA

Your device's camera can be accessed in a number of ways. Your device might include a button, usually located somewhere along the outside edge, which is used to actually snap the pictures, but also can be pressed to simply launch the camera application, or you can launch it as you would any other application on your device.

After you launch the app, your screen should display whatever you happen to be pointing the camera at. On some devices, this is all you will see, but on others, you may have additional controls and options visible on-screen. At its simplest, taking a picture simply involves pointing your device's camera at the subject and pressing the camera button. The picture is saved automatically. On some devices, the new picture may appear briefly before you return to the camera view, while on others you will be taken back to the camera view immediately. If your device includes a flash, it will fire — or not — at the software's discretion.

VIEWING YOUR PICTURES

The fact that pictures are now free is, as I mentioned, one of the really great things about digital photography. Another great thing is the fact that you can view pictures instantly to see whether you really got the shot you were looking for. My kids take this for granted; every time someone points a camera at them, which is a lot because they are, of course, really cute kids, they expect to be able to walk — or more often run — over and see the picture right away.

Whether your device's camera displays the image for a few seconds or not, the most recently shot image will display as a small thumbnail in the bottom corner of the camera app while you prepare to snap the next photo. Simply select the thumbnail to display it. Depending on your device and the exact version of Android you are running, you either get the last photo full-screen, or some other display of your images. On some devices, the images appear in the so-called Camera Roll, which allows you to scroll through them with a cool animated effect. On others, each image may appear individually on-screen (see Figure 9.1).

Figure 9.1
The Droid X Camera Roll

You also can view your photos without going into the camera at all by using the Gallery application, one of the standard applications in all versions of Android. Once again, the exact details of what the Gallery displays vary between models and variants of Android, but the basics are the same: You see your images organized into some sort of folder structure. Usually, the pictures you have taken with your camera's device will be separate from pictures you may have downloaded off the web and separate from pictures you may have transferred from your computer. You can select each folder to display its images, and then select any image to display it full-screen.

Most devices automatically rotate pictures as you rotate your device, so that pictures with landscape orientation will shrink to fit the available space when you hold your device normally but rotate to display full-screen when you rotate your device (see

Figure 9.2). The opposite applies to pictures taken with a portrait orientation.

SHARING YOUR PICTURES

Any picture you take with your device can be shared instantly with others, using text messaging, Facebook, Twitter, or other applications.

Sharing with MMS

Although texting was, as the name implies, designed for text, the system has been expanded to now include the ability to transmit multimedia content such as pictures. Technically, it uses a slightly different technology known as MMS or Multimedia Messaging Service. Android enables you to very easily add a picture to a text message without worrying about which technology is being used.

If you want to text a picture you have just taken, you can do so directly within

Figure 9.2
Pictures automatically rotate with the device.

the Camera or Gallery app. When viewing the picture full-screen, press the device's Menu button and then select Share. You get another menu that lists the applications on your device capable of sharing pictures (see Figure 9.3); select Text Messaging.

TIP

An irony of newer devices is that they often take pictures too large to send via text message. Therefore, you may see a warning that the picture you are sending is too large and needs to be resized. Simply select Resize to have the application do this for you. Do not worry, though, as only the copy of the picture that is being sent is resized, and the original will remain untouched.

A standard text message window will open in which you can type the recipients to whom you want to send the picture and a note explaining it. When done, select Send.

Sharing on Facebook

Facebook originally was conceived as a service built around the idea of sharing pictures, and it has, in fact, become a common way for many people to share pictures of family, vacations, or important events. If you have the Facebook app installed on your device, it integrates with the Gallery to enable you to easily upload pictures you take with your device to Facebook. See Chapter 5 for details on installing and setting up the Facebook app on your device.

To begin, follow the steps outlined in the preceding section to select a picture and display the menu of photo-sharing services. This time, obviously, you want to select

Facebook. Doing so launches the Facebook app to the Upload photo section. You can type a caption for the photo and then select Upload. It may take a moment or two to upload the photo, but after you do, it will appear on your Wall and in the Photos section of your Facebook account.

Sharing on Twitter

The Twitter service itself allows you to post only short text messages of no more than 140 characters. Pictures and anything else are not supported. However, a number

Figure 9.3
The applications on my device that can be used to send pictures

of services have sprung up to enable Twitter users to upload their images and then post a link to the image on Twitter. Many of the Twitter clients even display the image automatically when viewing a tweet. See Chapter 5 for details on getting started with Twitter on your device.

To post a picture to Twitter using the official Twitter app, follow the steps outlined previously to select the picture and display the menu of applications that can share it. This time, select Twitter. The application automatically generates a link on the photo-sharing site Twitpic, which will be inserted into your Tweet (see Figure 9.4). Type any other text you want to add to the tweet — keeping in mind that the entire message, including the Twitpic link, must be no more than 140 characters — and select Update. The picture then is uploaded to Twitpic, and your tweet is posted for all of your followers to see.

Sharing via E-mail

You can also go old school and simply e-mail a picture to someone. If you have a person who has an older device that cannot directly accept MMS messages, or perhaps works in an environment that does not allow access to or use of devices, e-mailing remains a reliable sharing model.

Follow the steps outlined previously to select the picture, this time choosing either Email or Gmail as the sharing option, depending on which one you use. See Chapter 5 for details on both. Either way, a new message is generated with the picture added as an attachment. Simply enter the recipient addresses, a subject, and a message body, just as you would any other e-mail and select Send.

TIDBIT

If you are on a Mac, you may need to download the Android File Transfer application, available for free from http://www.android.com/filetransfer/ in order to transfer files directly between your device and your computer. This application will mount your device as a hard drive and allow you to drag and drop files.

Figure 9.4

Preparing to send a tweet with the link to Twitpic generated automatically

Other Sharing Methods

Your device may contain other applications that support sharing photos. For example, some Motorola devices include a social sharing application that connects to a number of social networks and enables you to post the picture to multiple networks at the same time. They also include an application that can connect to certain retail outlets to directly print your images.

DOWNLOADING PICTURES TO YOUR COMPUTER

In addition to sharing images electronically, you also can download your images to your desktop or laptop computer. To do this, you need to simply plug your device into your computer using USB. Then mount your SD card by pulling down the Notifications Bar and selecting USB Connection. Depending on your version of Android, you are either given a simple dialog box with the choice to mount your SD card or a more complex one with several options (see Figure 9.5). If you have the former, select the button to mount the card; if the latter, choose either PC Mode or USB Mass Storage, as either will work in this case. See Chapter 1 for a more thorough explanation of these options.

With the card mounted, your computer should automatically detect your device as a new hard drive. If you use Windows, you are shown a dialog box with a set of options for how to deal with the card. If you have a photo-editing or management tool installed on your computer such as Adobe Photoshop Elements, you should see an option to automatically import the photos into it, which is the easy way to download the images. If

Figure 9.5

SD card mounting options on the Droid X

you do not have a program that can import for you, select the option to open Windows Explorer.

If you need to manually download the images, you can simply use either Windows Explorer or Mac Finder to drag the images from the device's Albums folder to your hard drive.

FIND OUT WHERE YOU TOOK A PICTURE

Your phone and some tablets include a GPS device. Most of the time, we think of using GPS within Maps to find directions to places, as is covered in Chapter 7. However, many other applications can and do use GPS, including your camera. If enabled, the GPS function in your camera can record the latitude and longitude of every picture you take in a process known as geotagging. How is this useful? Well, it allows you to display a map on your device of the precise location for each picture, which can be particularly helpful when you are traveling and may end up taking pictures of fairly similar monuments or sites. After you transfer your pictures to your computer, you may have programs that can perform similar functions as well using the geotag embedded by your device.

Enabling GPS on Your Camera

Many newer models of devices come with geotagging enabled on the camera by default. Other cameras may need it to be turned on. The exact steps needed to enable the geotagging on the camera may also vary slightly, but in general they will be located in either the settings or tags sections of the menu. On the Droid X, you can turn geotagging on or off by pressing the Menu button on the device, selecting Tags, and then either checking or unchecking the Auto Location Tag setting (see Figure 9.6).

When taking pictures on the Droid X, for example, you can tell whether geotagging is on by looking in the top-left corner of the screen when you first launch the camera. If enabled, you will see a small tag icon and, for a few seconds, your current location. If the location has disappeared, you can tap the tag icon to display it again.

TIP

Geotagging on your camera suffers from the same shortcomings as any GPS-enabled application: Your device must have a clear line of sight to one of the GPS satellites, which in the Northern Hemisphere generally means a line of sight to the southern sky. Thus, pictures taken inside will not generally get tagged, as will other pictures taken when the signal might be blocked, such as downtown in large cities. Also, be aware that your camera and GPS are, independently, two of the biggest drains on battery power, so combining them means that you will lose power much faster than normal if you are taking a lot of pictures.

Using Geotagging on Your Device

After you have taken pictures with geotagging enabled, you can display the latitude and longitude by bringing up a picture in the Gallery, selecting the menu arrow (the white arrow in a circle in the bottom-right corner of the screen), then selecting Picture info. This will display details about the image, including the location where it was taken (see Figure 9.7). From the same information screen, you can select the Maps icon to the left of the coordinates to launch your Maps application and see where you took the picture.

EDIT PICTURES ON YOUR DEVICE

For more than 20 years, Adobe Photoshop has been the industry-standard photo-editing tool. The desktop application, while extremely powerful, is unfor-

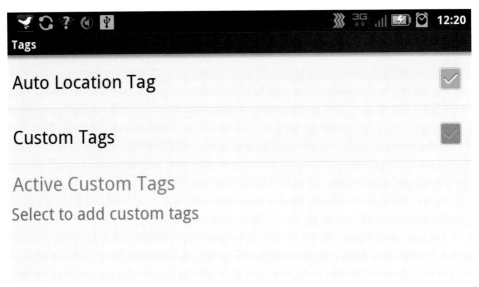

Figure 9.6
Enabling or disabling geotagging with the Auto Location Tag setting

TIP

Computers are primarily sold by throwing a bunch of numbers at unsuspecting customers, hoping that they will not know or really worry about what those numbers mean. Just about everyone has a vague sense that somehow higher numbers are better. Digital cameras suffer from this as well, but unfortunately, the big number everyone discusses is something of a red herring: megapixels. Walk into any electronics or photography store, and you will hear the word thrown about with reckless abandon, but ask the people in the store — customers and salespeople alike — what it actually means, and you will likely get a bunch of half-mumbled responses that, in the end, all translate to "I don't know." So then, what is it? Well, your computer's display is sort of like a big sheet of graph paper, and each little square on the graph is known as a pixel. Mega is the prefix for a million, so in literal terms a megapixel is a million pixels. How this relates to photography is that every image is a rectangle made up of pixels, so megapixels describe the size of the image: An image that is 1000 pixels wide by 1000 pixels tall would contain 1 million pixels and would, thus, be 1 megapixel. The number of megapixels associated with a camera, therefore, describes the maximum size of image the camera can take. Why, then, did I describe this as a red herring? Well, because ultimately, to quote Yoda, "Size matters not." Lots of megapixels means that you are getting big pictures, but that does not necessarily mean that you are getting good pictures. Two much more important factors govern the quality of images, neither of which has changed in the slightest since the camera's invention roughly 150 years ago: the quality of the optics in the camera, and even more important, the quality of the photographer behind it. Only time and practice can improve the second factor, but consider the first the next time you buy a camera: A 6-megapixel camera with really good optics will beat a 12-megapixel camera with bad optics every single time.

tunately quite expensive. Fortunately, however, you can now leverage much of the power of Photoshop directly on your device absolutely free. You can download the Photoshop Express application from the Android Market. Once installed and launched, it will display all of the images on your device (see Figure 9.8).

Choose any image to display it full-screen. Then press your device's Menu button and select Edit Photo (see Figure 9.9). You can also press the Edit button at the bottom of the app window and then choose the image

you want to edit. This will reload the image, this time including a set of tools both above and below.

The first of the tools along the top is the Crop tool. Selecting the tool displays a menu of tools, including Crop, Straighten, Rotate, and Flip. Cropping enables you to cut away areas of the image to either make it smaller or to focus your viewer's attention on some particular part of the image. When you select the tool, you will see the image with a box highlighting the area to be saved. You can drag to resize or move

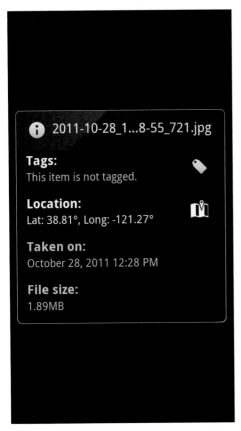

Figure 9.7

The information screen for one of my pictures, showing the coordinates at which it was shot

Figure 9.8

Photoshop Express loaded on the device

this crop area. The lock icon at the bottom of the screen allows you to maintain the image's aspect ratio as you crop. After you have the area you want to save selected, simply select the green check mark, which returns you to the editing window. You can also select the red circle with the X to cancel your edits and return to the Edit window.

The Straighten, Rotate, and Flip tools all do exactly what they say. If you take a picture when you are not holding the camera

perfectly level, you can use the Straighten tool to correct your mistake. The Rotate tool spins your image in 90-degree increments, which can be helpful if you are planning to upload your image to a service such as Facebook.com that will not automatically rotate pictures taken in the portrait orientation. The Flip tool flips your photo either horizontally or vertically. As with the Crop tool, you can select the green check mark to apply your changes or the red X to cancel them, each returning you to the Edit screen.

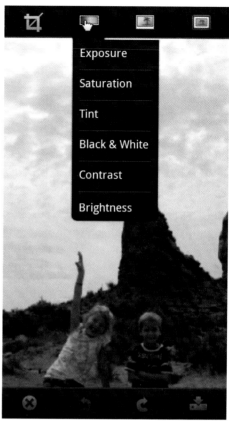

Figure 9.9

Preparing to edit the image

Figure 9.10

The menu of options for editing your image

Reword to this: You can make adjustments to the image using the tool as displayed in Figure 9.10. Selecting this tool gives you choices for Exposure, Saturation, Tint, Black and White, Contrast and Brightness. (see Figure 9.10). All except the Black & White tool work in essentially the same way, enabling you to drag your finger on the image to either increase or decrease the effect of the tool. Exposure changes the overall lightness or darkness of the image. Saturation either increases or decreases the amount of color in the picture, and Tint changes the overall colors (see Figure 9.11). Contrast and Bright-

ness, like Exposure, change the lightness and darkness of the image, but whereas Exposure affects the overall image, Contrast only lightens or darkens the shadows of the image, while Brightness affects the highlights. The final tool in the set, Black & White, does what it says: It converts your image to black and white. It does not have any adjustable settings.

The final two top menus apply effects. The first button applies a soft focus filter to your image, which you can adjust by dragging (see Figure 9.12). The second displays a

Figure 9.11
Changing the tint of the image

Figure 9.12
Applying the Soft Focus filter

menu with an option to apply other effects and one to apply borders. The effects include filters such as Vignette Blur and Soft Black & White; it is really easiest to simply play with these on images to see the effect. Borders enable you to apply a border such as simple white lines or an old film emulsion look.

The options along the bottom of the screen, from left to right, enable you to cancel all edits you have made to the image, undo your last edit, redo your last edit, or save the image. A very nice feature of the program is that it always saves your edits to a copy of the image, so you can really do whatever you want to a picture and not worry about ruining the original.

After you complete your editing and either save or cancel, you are returned to the main app screen. From here, you can upload your image to the Photoshop.com website, Facebook, or Twitpic, where you can easily share your pictures with others. The Photoshop.com website requires that you create a free account before you can upload images; when you select the Upload button and select Photoshop.com, you are given the choice of either logging

into your existing account or creating a
new one.

If you have or create a Photoshop.com
account, you can access any photos you have
uploaded via the Online tab at the top of
the applications main screen. You can view
these images and set them as your device's
wallpaper, but you cannot directly edit
them.

Video

The Skim

am an unapologetic film buff. A friend recently asked what I thought was the single worst movie I have ever seen, and honestly, it was a question I could not easily answer. That was not to say that I have not seen any bad movies, but rather, that I have seen far too many bad movies to be able to pick out any one in particular. I really will see almost anything and have on more than one occasion simply showed up at a theater and bought a ticket for whatever happened to be starting next. (He knew he did not need to ask what my favorite movie was, because you need only spend a little time with me to discover my undying devotion to Joss Whedon's *Serenity*. In fact, you do not even need to get to know me, because I do manage to throw at least a few references to the movie or the TV show upon which it was based into every one of my books.) Given this love of film, it should be no great surprise to find that I like shooting video as well. Growing up, video cameras were too bulky and far too expensive to be anything more than a novelty to many, but today, the same factors that have pushed the astronomical rise in still photography have begun to apply to video. Cameras are smaller and cheaper than ever before and have become progressively easier to use. Android phones have, from fairly early on, included the ability to capture video, but many of today's models — and most every tablet — include cameras capable of capturing video in high definition.

CAPTURING VIDEO ON YOUR DEVICE

Depending on your model of device and your variant of Android, the exact name of your video application may vary. You can also access the video camera by going into your device's regular camera and finding the button, displayed somewhere on the screen, that switches the camera's mode to video.

Either way, once you are in the camera you can simply point and shoot: Press the same button on the camera you use for taking a picture to start recording, and then press that same button again to stop. Some

models allow you to zoom in and out on the video while shooting. Many devices use the volume buttons for this, but instructions on zooming should display on the camera when you first launch it.

You do have a limited amount of time you can shoot. For all the advances in video, one big hurdle remains: video files are huge. Thus, you will find that you can fill your SD card quite quickly if you use the video camera a lot; plan to download the video to your computer frequently. Your device may also impose a limit on each video; on the Droid X, for example, you are limited to 30 minutes per shot.

VIEWING YOUR VIDEOS

You can watch your movies as soon as you shoot them by selecting the screen immediately after stopping the video and then pressing the Play button (see Figure 10.1). Videos are also available via the Gallery, alongside your photos (see Figure 10.2).

On some newer devices, you may be able to play a video directly on your TV. Models including the Droid X, Droid X2, and Xoom tablet include an HDMI jack. If your device includes the jack and you have a high-definition TV, you can purchase an HDMI cable for your device from your local electronics store and then plug the device in and play video.

SHARING YOUR VIDEO

If you would like others to see your cinematic masterpiece, you can easily upload your video to YouTube from your device. From the Gallery, select the video to open it, then press the Menu button and select Share. From the resulting menu, select YouTube (see Figure 10.3). You can add a title

TIP

Unless you are intentionally trying to shoot video in the style of *The Blair Witch Project*, you should try as best as possible to remain still while shooting. Along the same lines, if you are going to zoom in or out, do so slowly. While underlighting worked well for Ingmar Bergman, you will likely find that the better the lighting in the area you are shooting, the better your movie will look. If your device includes a flash, you will be able to select the Light button on the camera app to turn on the flash, but be aware that this will cause a significant strain on the battery.

Figure 10.1
Play a video by pressing the play button — the large triangle in the middle of the screen.

Figure 10.2
Videos in the Gallery

to your video and select More details to add a location and set the video to either Public or Private (see Figure 10.4). If you select Pub-

lic, the video will appear on the YouTube site for all to see; if Private, only you will be able to view it by logging into YouTube.

Figure 10.3
Sharing your video via YouTube

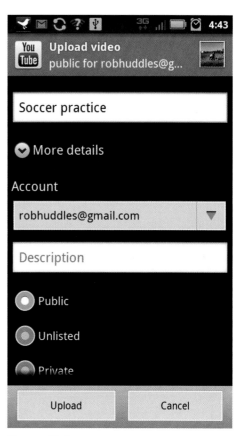

Figure 10.4
Setting the details on the video

TIP

You may not know this, but you already have a YouTube account. Several years ago, Google bought the video sharing service after attempting, and failing, to create a competitor, so the same Google account you needed to create in order to start using your phone works on YouTube.

Once the video has been uploaded, you can continue to view it on your device via the Gallery or with the YouTube application that comes as a standard part of Android. You can also view it online via the YouTube website (see Figure 10.5).

PREPARING A VIDEO TO UPLOAD TO YOUR PHONE

In addition to shooting and watching your own videos, you can also upload videos from your computer to your phone. In order to do this, however, you need to do a few things to the video on your computer first.

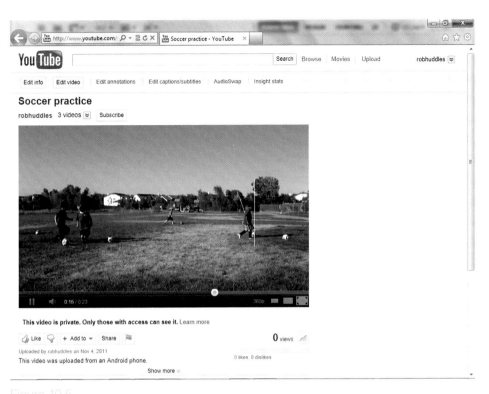

Figure 10.5
Viewing a video shot on my phone on YouTube

Of course, the very first step is to make sure that it is legally okay to convert and upload the video you are trying to use. In very broad terms, you should be able to transfer videos you purchase or download online to your phone, so long as you do not plan to use that video for any public viewing. Store-bought videos such as DVD or Blu-ray discs, may have additional restrictions, but many newer movies include a digital copy expressly for this purpose. If you have one of those, you can pretty much skip this entire section, because the digital copy will already be all set for transferring to your phone.

Once you are sure you can use the video, you may need to convert it to the proper format. According to Google, Android supports movies in 3GP and MP4 formats, but they do include a nice little caveat that devices "may provide support for additional formats or file types." I , for example, played AVI files on my Droid X with no problems. So there are two bits of bad news here: First, there is a pretty good chance that whatever format your video is in, it will be wrong; and second, there is no easy, sure-fire way to know that. The good news is that you can, fairly easily, convert video from one format to another, albeit with a few caveats. While I cannot say with any certainty what format your particular device does or does not support, I can tell you two formats that it most definitely will not: DVD and Blu-ray.

Technically, neither of those is a format per se, but the point is that you can definitely not expect to put a DVD into your computer's drive and find a file to drag onto your phone and expect it to play. Those you will definitely have to convert, assuming that they are not encrypted. You will need some software on your machine to perform the conversion for you. Here again is good news, as a handy piece of software has been created for just this purpose: Handbrake. It is able to convert video from almost any format to almost any other format, completely free, and both look and act identical on both Windows and Mac. Download Handbrake from http://handbrake.fr/downloads.php and install it. Once complete, launch the program (see Figure 10.6).

Click the Source button in the top-left corner and select the video you wish to convert. If you need to convert a video you already have on your computer into a different format, select Video file; if you are going to try to convert a DVD, select that option. Then select the format into which you wish to convert; remember, for Android you want MP4. Then click the Video tab and select H.264 from the Video Codec drop-down list (see Figure 10.7). Next, go to the Picture tab and change the Anamorphic setting to loose, which will allow you to manually enter a size for the video. Go up to the Width text box just above that and enter the width of your screen; if you do not know what it is, you should be able to look it up on Google by searching on your phone and the words "screen resolution." For example, typing "Droid X screen resolution" tells me that my screen is 480 x 854, so I would set the width to 854 or less — note that you cannot size videos up in Handbrake, so if the width is already less than your resolution, you should leave it at its original size (see Figure 10.8). Finally, click Start (see Figure 10.9). Be aware that video compression can be very slow, so you will need to be patient.

TIP

Handbrake can do a fine job ripping non-copyright-protected DVDs, but what about ones that are protected? And hey, it is the twenty-first century, so how about Blu-ray? Well, Handbrake cannot handle encrypted DVDs without some help, and it cannot deal with Blu-ray at all. It is possible to decrypt copy-protected DVDs, but the legality of doing so, particularly in the United States, is still in the realm of things being argued by lawyers and judges. If you are interested in doing it anyway, there are plenty of resources online to walk you through it. As for Blu-ray: These are the discs where you are likely to find a digital copy, so you may be in luck. If not, you can read instructions for ripping a Blu-ray disc at http://gizmodo.com/5161848/how-to-rip-blu+ray-discs; note the important point the site makes that it takes a very long time to rip Blu-ray discs.

UPLOAD A VIDEO TO YOUR PHONE

You can upload videos from your computer to your phone exactly as you would any other file. Plug the phone into your USB port and mount the SD card by pulling down the Notifications Bar, selecting USB Connection, and either Mount SD Card, PC Mode, or USB Mass Storage; any will work. Once mounted, your phone will appear on your computer as an additional drive. Navigate to the Video folder on the card and drag your movie there. Then unmount the card by clicking the icon on your task tray in Windows and selecting either Eject or Stop, or on a Mac by dragging the drive to the trash can. On your phone, pull down the Notifications Bar and select Unmount. Keep in mind that video files can be quite large, so you will need to be sure that you have enough space on your SD card for them.

Once you have the video transferred to your phone, you will find it in the Gallery in

ALTERNATE APP

You have to be able to save the time needed to convert your videos by downloading QQPlayer, a free app available in the Market that allows you to play a much wider variety of video files. I have had mixed success with QQPlayer, however: While all videos play, I have found times when the audio and video get out of sync. In those cases, I go ahead and use Handbrake.

a folder labeled either "Videos" or "Movies" (see Figure 10.10). You can play these videos exactly as you would any other: Simply

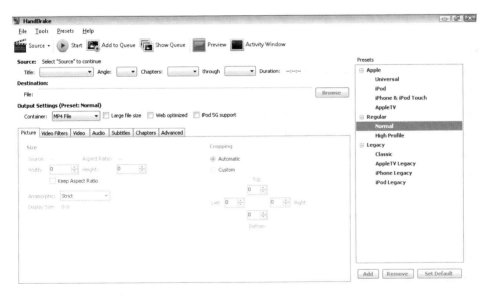

Figure 10.6

Handbrake on Windows; a Mac version is also available and is identical in both look and function. And no, I have no idea what the cocktail glass and pineapple represent.

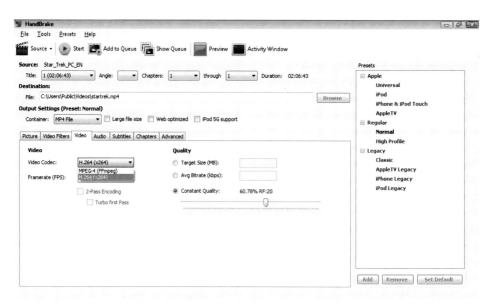

Figure 10.7

Specifying video settings for the conversion

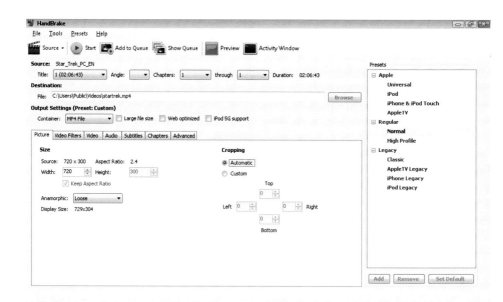

Figure 10.8

Setting the resolution

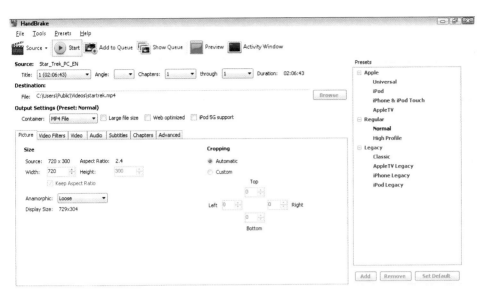

Figure 10.9
Starting the conversion

Figure 10.10
A movie copied from my computer to the phone appearing in the Gallery

select it in the gallery to begin playing. A set of playback controls will appear for a few seconds when the movie starts with a pause button and a slider that allows you to move to any part of the movie; you can get these controls back at any time by double-tapping on the screen.

WATCH STREAMING CONTENT ON YOUR DEVICE

Going through the trouble to download and convert videos and TV shows to load on your device is great if you are on a limited data plan or going to be somewhere for an extended period of time without data, such as a long flight. Much of the time, however, you will be in range of a signal, either via 3G or (if your device supports it) 4G, or Wi-Fi. In these cases, you have access to an ever-

growing list of resources that can stream content directly to your device.

Google

In 2011, Google began offering streaming movie rentals through the Market. Unlike its major competitors like Netflix and Blockbuster, where you can pay a monthly subscription fee to enjoy unlimited streaming, Google offers a more traditional rental-on-demand model where you pay by movie. The good news about this plan is that Hollywood seems to like it better, and is offering recent releases of big movies that you are unlikely to find on Netflix or Blockbuster until much later (see Figure 10.11). Most movies are between $2-4.

You can access the Google movie library by simply opening the Market and selecting Movies. You can browse by category, popularity, or new releases, or, of course you can search for a particular title.

Netflix

Long the leader in mail-order DVD rentals, Netflix has over the last few years moved increasingly into streaming content. Despite its well-publicized missteps in 2011, Netflix remains a strong contender in the market and is the default streaming content provider in the minds of many users.

If you are a Netflix subscriber, you can access its streaming library directly on your phone or on some tablets. The list of tablets that Netflix supports is ever expanding, but it is not all-inclusive; if watching streaming content is one of your primary reasons for considering the purchase of a tablet, you may want to check and make sure that Netflix supports the model you plan to buy.

NOTE

Be careful with any streaming media if you have a limited data plan, as all streaming content will use a lot of bandwidth and can very quickly use up your monthly allotment. If at all possible, users on limited data plans should try to limit consumption of streaming media to those times when you are on Wi-Fi instead. If watching streaming content on your device is a big consideration for you, then consider getting on an unlimited plan from the start. At least in the United States, Sprint is the only national service provider that currently offers unlimited data plans to new customers, although a lot of older Verizon, AT&T, and T-Mobile users may be grandfathered in on unlimited plans.

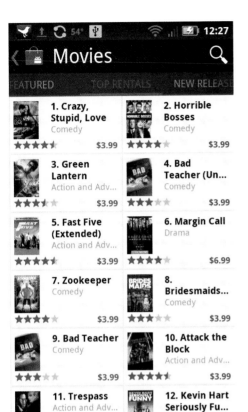

Blockbuster, for years far and away the biggest video rental chain, was slow to recognize the threat posed by Netflix, but it has been much quicker to respond to the change in its business caused by the rise of streaming video, and while its retail locations continue to disappear, the company remains a strong competitor in the streaming video market.

Using the same basic model as Netflix, you can sign up for a monthly plan with Blockbuster to access its streaming library.

Figure 10.11
The Google Market Top Rentals section

Getting started with Netflix is as simple as downloading and installing the Netflix app from the Android Market, then signing in with your current Netflix streaming account credentials. Once you are logged in, using the service on your device is very similar to using it on your TV: You can browse your streaming queue or simply search for a title. The quality of the streaming video will vary depending on the quality of the signal, but most of the times I have used it the picture and sound have been very good (see Figure 10.12).

TIDBIT

Search the forums of most every Android site and you will find a common theme: users of devices that came with the Blockbuster app preinstalled who want to remove it. Unfortunately, part of the agreement that Blockbuster makes with providers is that the app needs to be protected and not available to uninstall like other apps. The Blockbuster app is not the only app that falls into this category.

The good news is that, if you really, really want to uninstall Blockbuster and any other preinstalled apps, it is technically possible. The bad news is that it requires that you root your device, which can be a tricky process, and might prevent your device from being updated. As the process of rooting your device varies wildly from one device to the next, it is not covered in this book, but those same forums should provide you with ample links to step you through the process.

Blockbuster was much faster to realize the potential of offering streaming content to devices, and has made an app available for Android for several years. In fact, much to the chagrin of many users, the Blockbuster app comes preinstalled with many devices. If it is not already on your phone, it can be downloaded from the Market. Like Netflix, the app is free, but you need to subscribe to access content.

Amazon

Seeking to compete with Netflix, Blockbuster and others, Amazon now offers streaming videos as well. Its streaming catalog is offered to those who sign up for their premium Amazon Prime service, which as of this writing costs $79 per year. Amazon Prime includes a lot of other services — free overnight shipping being my personal favor-

ite —so getting free movies on top of everything else makes Prime a pretty good deal.

As of now, Amazon has not developed an app for its streaming movies, but its player is built on Adobe Flash, and since Flash is supported on Android, you can use your device's browser to watch movies on Amazon (see Figure 10.13).

Hulu Plus

A surprisingly large number of my friends have, over the last year or so, dumped their cable or satellite services and switched to watching TV shows online, thanks mostly to Hulu. You cannot watch shows live via the service, but I honestly know very few people who watch TV live anymore even when connecting through cable and satellite, thanks to DVRs. Hulu instead provides a wide array of TV shows, both new and old,

Figure 10.12

Watching Netflix on the Xoom

Figure 10.13

Accessing Amazon's streaming movies via the browser

streaming online. Much of the content is free, while additional programming is available via a paid subscription service known as Hulu Plus.

If you are a fan of Hulu, you may be pleased to know that you can get Hulu on your device thanks to the Hulu Plus app. Note the name, however: The app provides access to the premium Hulu Plus service. The free content is available through Hulu Plus as well, but you are going to have to pay for access. (The app is free, by the way: it's the service you are paying for.) Still, the fee is relatively small, and if you really want to view the latest exploits of Richard Castle within a day or so of the show airing on TV, Hulu Plus is the way to go.

HBO and Cinemax

Premium cable providers HBO and Cinemax (which are both owned by HBO) now make many of their programs available via streaming to their customers. Availability varies based on your cable or satellite provider, so not all HBO/Cinemax customers may have access, but if you do, this is a great way to catch up on *Game of Thrones* or watch that Cinemax movie you missed over the weekend.

HBO offers streaming on devices through an app called HBOGo. The app is currently available on a wide variety of phones and an increasing number of tablets, but as with Netflix, you will need to check to make sure your device is supported.

Assuming that you can download the app, and assuming that your cable or satellite provider has agreed to whatever terms it is that HBO requires, you can simply log in — although note that you actually log in via your cable or satellite provider, not HBO, so you may need to create an online account with your provider — and access HBO's content.

What is particularly nice about HBOGo is that you can watch all of those great shows that it produce these days, such as *Sopranos, Deadwood, Game of Thrones*, and more (see Figure 10.14). It also gives you access to a variety of movies, although the availability of the movies changes, so if you see one you want to watch, watch it right away since it might not be there the next time you log in.

While accessing HBO via the app is great, there are still a lot of devices out there that the app doesn't support. Thankfully, all is not lost, as you can also access HBOGo via

Figure 10.14

Game of Thrones on a phone, thanks to HBOGo

the browser, which seems to work on all devices. Simply open your device's browser and navigate to http://www.hbogo.com. Log in with your username and password from your cable or satellite provider, and you can get all of the same content you can through the app.

Cinemax has yet to release an app, but just like HBOGo, its content is available through the web. Use your device's browser to go to http://www.maxgo.com. All of the same restrictions apply to Cinemax as apply to HBO — it is, after all, the same company — so you need to actually log in through your cable or satellite provider. The good news is that this does mean that you can log in with the same credentials you use to access HBOGo. Cinemax is, at this time, almost all movies, and just like HBO, its selection is constantly changing.

VIDEO CHAT

While we are still waiting for flying cars and robot maids, we do have one Jetsons invention available to us today: video chat. Several solutions for video chat have existed for some time, but they suffered from one major drawback: Many Android phones only have a camera on the back, so you cannot look at the screen and take a picture of yourself at the same time. This problem was solved with the current generation of tablets (and an increasing number of phones) that have both front- and rear-facing cameras. This is perhaps the best use for that front-facing camera — most other uses that come to mind are a bit creepy. A few limitations still exist on video chat, though: In order for the system to work, you need someone on the other end of the line that also has a device with a front-facing camera or who is sitting at a computer with a webcam; and both of you must be on the same system.

Google Talk

Google added video chat to its Talk app in an update in early 2011. Since then, it has been very slow to push the update to phones, so while the Nexus S and some tablets have it, almost all phones still lack the feature, and tablet support is spotty. The lack of phone support is not quite as big a deal as some online like to make it; as was mentioned previously, video chat on any device without a front-facing camera is practically useless anyway, so most phones lack the hardware needed to make the feature really workable anyway.

You can test to see if your device supports video chat by simply opening the Talk app. A small green video camera icon will appear next to some of your contact's names if you have the feature. Simply tap the icon and, assuming the contact is available and accepts your chat request, you will be connected.

Skype

Skype, in case you are one of the few who don't already use it, is a popular service that allows you to make calls on your computer, either to other Skype users or to physical phones. Skype on Android is a mixed bag, depending on your carrier. For many, Skype was probably their first experience with video chat, as the company has offered it in its desktop app for quite some time.

First, a brief bit of history. When Skype first developed its Android app, it had an exclusive deal with Verizon. In fact, for a time Skype on Android was not only available only to Verizon customers, but it was in fact one of the apps that came preinstalled on phones. That was great, assuming that you were a Verizon customer, and assuming you were okay with the big limitation Verizon imposed on its Skype app, restricting its use only to Verizon's data plan and disabling it on Wi-Fi. It was obviously a good deal for Verizon: It potentially picked up customers to whom availability of Skype on the phone was a major selling point.

Over time, however, the deal soured, and now Skype is available in the Android Market to all Android users. What is even better is that the version in the Market removes the no-Wi-Fi restriction, meaning that users who are on limited data plans need not use up most, if not all, of their monthly allotment on a single call. Again, good news — unless you are a Verizon customer. It turns out that having access to Skype before customers on other carriers is turning out to be not such a great deal, as the Verizon version continues to disable access on Wi-Fi.

In addition, while video chat is a standard part of the desktop version of Skype, it is not yet available across the board in the Android version, so once you download and install the app, you will need to check to see if video chat is available. This is really just a matter of time, however; one can presume that the company is working on getting the feature into all versions.

In 2011, by the way, Microsoft purchased Skype. Very little has been revealed about the company's plans for the service, but it will be interesting to see what changes come about as the software giant integrates Skype into its product line. As Microsoft has no other Android apps available, there is really no telling which way it might go.

GOOGLETV: ANDROID ON YOUR TV

Originally, computer monitors were little more than glorified TV screens. Today, that has been reversed, and most TVs today contain an increasing array of features that bring the internet to the TV.

In late 2010, Google announced a new venture: GoogleTV. The idea was to provide a unique feature set for the television. Initially, two versions of GoogleTV were available: the Logitech Revue, a set-top box that you plugged in between your satellite or cable signal and your TV and interacted with via wireless keyboard (see Figure 10.15), and a Sony set that integrated the GoogleTV features directly into the television set.

GoogleTV is Android. You certainly would not guess it from looking at the ser-

vice, as the user interface is nothing like any other version of Android out there, at least in part because it is designed for keyboard interaction instead of touch.

GoogleTV was released to mixed reviews. The biggest complaint was that the major network providers and many streaming online services such as Hulu immediately blocked access from GoogleTV. Thankfully, many other providers reached agreement with Google, so services such as HBOGo and Netflix are available.

Personally, I think those reviews missed the mark. As far as I can tell—and I have had a Logitech Revue since about a month after it was released—the service was never intended as a replacement for your satellite or cable provider. Instead, I look at it as more of an enhancement. I get my TV sig-

Figure 10.15

The Logitech Revue and keyboard

nal via Dish Network, and the Dish inter-face that I use to view the programming guide and watch shows on my DVR is, to put it nicely, horrible. Using GoogleTV, I can more quickly find shows I want to watch, thanks to the built-in search fea-ture. The search is even nice enough to look not only on what is on currently, but also in my DVR, so for instance if I search for *Phineas and Ferb*, it will not only bring up the listing of when that fantastic show airs next on the Disney XD channel, but it will also display my saved recording of the recent *Phineas and Ferb* movie. You can even search by actor or description, not just show title. Using the keyboard, I can set an upcoming show to record in my DVR with a single click. The keyboard allows me to turn my TV on and off and control the volume, essentially eliminat-ing two remotes. Oh, and because the keyboard connects to the box via Wi-Fi, I don't have to worry about being in a line of sight the way I do with traditional remotes. I can even use my phone and tablet to con-trol the service through the free Logitech Revue app, available in the Market (see Figure 10.16).

Obviously, I am a bit of a fan of GoogleTV, which makes it that much more difficult to accept how badly Google ignored it. Sales of the Revue were nowhere near what Google or Logitech wanted, and as far as I know even fewer of the Sony units ever sold. As such, updates to the system were few and far between for its first year. Thankfully, the end of 2011 brought with it the long-awaited update to GoogleTV. The update includes an all-new interface and, at long last, access to the Market and apps. Initially, Market access is somewhat limited, but for the most part the limits make sense, as, for example, blocking apps that rely solely on touch for their interface.

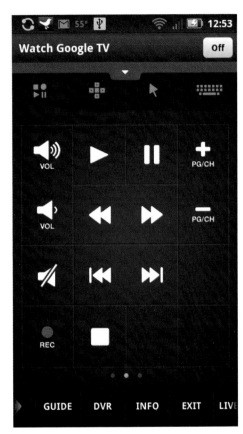

Figure 10.16

The Logitech Revue remote control app on my phone

The Web

The Skim

ew technologies have changed the world as quickly as the web. While the inventions of the wheel, the printing press, and sliced bread might, in the bigger sense, be more important, none took hold of our collective consciousness as quickly as the web, which in 2010 was only 20 years old. Equally as interesting is the fact that no one saw the web coming. In the 1960s, *Star Trek* predicted an impressive array of modern technology, including mobile phones and portable computers, but if you go back and rewatch the whole series, you will never hear Mr. Spock tell Captain Kirk that, rather than asking about the capabilities of that Romulan ship or whether that planet is habitable, he could just Google it.

While having the entirety of human knowledge at your fingertips is pretty cool, we were, for most of the web's existence, limited to looking things up on a heavy desktop computer that was inconveniently attached to the wall via cables. Wi-Fi let us break free of the cables, and now our mobile devices take us a step further, allowing access to the web literally anywhere.

SURFING THE WEB ON YOUR DEVICE

All Android devices include a browser, which is built on the open-source Webkit browser engine. Most likely, your carrier placed a shortcut to the browser directly on the home screen, but, of course, it is available in the Application Launcher. By default, your home page is a search engine. In many cases it will, not too surprisingly, be Google.

The behavior of the browser varies from one version of Android to the next. On some devices, pages will appear full size, with buttons in the lower corner that allow you to zoom in and out. Newer models contain a browser that displays pages zoomed out by default, so that you can see the entire page at a glance, and then either allow you to zoom in by pressing buttons or allow you to zoom by pinching the screen. You can also zoom in to view the page full size on the page by double-tapping anywhere on the screen, and zoom back out to see the entire page by double-tapping again.

You can navigate to pages in the same way you would on a traditional desktop browser. You can type the address of the site you wish to visit in the address bar at the top of the browser, and then select Go (see Figure 11.1). As you type, you will get suggestions for websites that match what you type, both from your favorites and history as well as Google's search. If the site you are looking for appears in the suggestions, you can simply select it to save typing the rest of the address.

SEARCHING THE WEB

As you are using a device running an operating system made by Google, the fact that you can easily search the web from your device should come as no surprise. You actually have a variety of ways that you can perform a search.

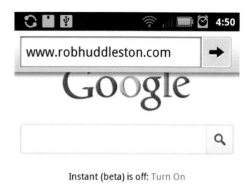

Figure 11.1

Opening a web page by typing its address in the browser's address bar

Searching the Old-Fashioned Way

Of course, you can use your device's browser to navigate to Google, type the term on which you wish to search, and choose the search button — the magnifying glass to the right of the search field. This will display the results just as they would on your computer.

Limiting Search Results

You can limit your search results to a particular region by adding a locale to the search. For example, a search for "pizza" will return millions of results related to all things pizza, but a search for "pizza, San Francisco, CA" will return a list, and map, of the pizza restaurants in San Francisco. A search for "pizza near me" will return a list of the restaurants near your current location (see Figure 11.2). You can limit your search to a specific website by including it in the results as well, so a search for "Android" returns a massive amount of sites devoted to Android, while a search for "Android site:wiley.com" returns a much more focused list of books and articles related to Android on this the publisher of this book's website.

Google search can also serve as a calculator by simply typing a mathematical expression in the search box. You can perform unit conversion by typing something like "1 cup in tablespoons", "350 Euros in US dollars", or "78 degrees Fahrenheit in degrees Celsius". Best of all, none of the techniques here is limited to your device — they all work in Google on the desktop as well.

Search without Returning to Google

If you are currently viewing some other page on your phone's browser and need to search for something, you do not need to return to Google's home page. Instead, you can press your phone's Search button, which will display the browser's address bar. Type the phrase on which you wish to search and press Go. The browser will send the term to Google and the results page will appear.

Voice Search in the Browser

On your phone, you can also talk to perform a search. Select the microphone

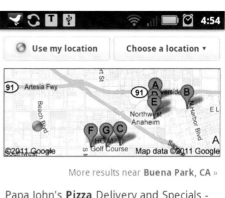

More results near **Buena Park, CA** »

Papa John's Pizza Delivery and Specials - Order Pizza Online for ...
Order Papa John's **Pizza** online for fast **pizza** delivery or pickup. Get Papa John's Special Offers or use Papa John's promo codes for ...
Find a Store - Order Now - Menu - Special Offers
www.papajohns.com/ - Options ▾

1179 North Euclid Street, Anaheim

2 Google reviews

| (714) 635-7272 | Map | Directions |

Pizza Delivery, Order Pizza Online, Dinner Deals, Catering - Pizza Hut
Order **pizza** online for fast **pizza** delivery or drop by for carryout. You may also contact **Pizza** Hut and find out about our catering ...

Figure 11.2

Results targeted near your current location

icon to the right of the address bar on the browser to bring up the voice search box, and then say the term or terms on which you wish to search. This will display the results of your search in the Voice Search application, from which you can choose any link to open the page in the browser.

Search Outside the Browser

Both text-based and voice search are available anytime on your phone, without first launching your browser. From your home screen, you can press your phone's

Search button to display a search field into which you can type a search term; pressing the search icon will launch your browser to the Google search results page.

Voice search is available from the same search box; instead of typing the phrase on which you wish to search, simply select the microphone icon and say your search phrase instead. You can also access the Voice Search application directly in your Application Launcher.

On a Honeycomb tablet, you can access search and voice search from the home screen. The top-left corner of the screen displays a magnifying glass and "Google", which you can select to open a search box. Just to the right of these icons is a microphone icon, which you can select to open voice search.

A home screen widget for search is also available. On Gingerbread and earlier, long-press on your home screen, select Widgets or Android Widgets, and then select Google Search. From the menu of search options

TIDBIT

Prior to Adobe's release of Flash Player 10.1 for Android, some Android phones were able to access limited Flash content via the Flash Lite player. Flash Lite was developed in the early days of web-capable phones. If you are on a phone running Android 2.1, you may be able to download and install Flash Lite, but be aware that many Flash-based sites will not work on Flash Lite.

that appears, you can select either All, Web, or Apps to determine what is searched.

USE FLASH PLAYER TO VIEW THE WHOLE WEB

Adobe Flash Player is the most-installed software in history, currently residing on more than 99 percent of all Internet-connected desktop and laptop computers. Its ubiquity has led to its adoption on a wide array of websites, from ads to games to video.

Flash is not installed on nearly as many mobile devices, but its presence in the mobile space is expanding rapidly. Any Android device, whether a phone or tablet, running at least Android 2.2 (FroYo) can install Flash. In fact, most of the Android phones and tablets that have shipped in the last year have Flash preinstalled. If you are unsure whether your device has it, the easiest way to check is to simply visit a website that uses Flash, such as www.adobe.com. If you see animated content, you have Flash and can go ahead and enjoy the whole web. If not, simply go to the Market and download it (see Figure 11.3).

USING BROWSER WINDOWS ON YOUR PHONE

You can have more than one web page open at a time on your phone by using browser windows. You can open a new window by pressing the phone's Menu button while on the browser and selecting New window. This will appear to reload the browser, returning you to your home page, from which point you can either navigate directly to a new site or search again.

You can press the Menu button and select Windows to see a list of all of the windows you currently have open. Select any of them to return to that window, or select the minus to close the window. You can also open another new window from this screen.

You are limited as to the number of windows you can have open at once. Be aware that some websites open links in new windows by default, so you may have windows open of which you are not aware. Also, if you reach your maximum number of windows and attempt to tap a link on a page that opens in a new window, the browser will display an error message. You will need to manually close some of your windows in order to follow the link.

Using Browser Tabs on Your Tablet

The version of the browser that ships with Honeycomb more closely resembles most modern desktop browsers and supports tabs (see Figure 11.4). You can open a new tab by selecting the plus sign icon to the right of the last open tab. You are limited to having 16 tabs open at a time.

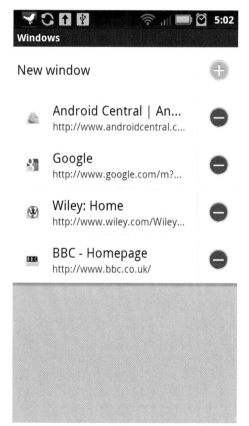

Figure 11.3
Flash content running on an Android phone

Figure 11.4
The windows currently open in my browser

BOOKMARK SITES

Just as you can on a desktop browser, you can save a reference to a site as a bookmark to make it easy to return to the site later. While viewing a site, you can press the bookmark icon on the browser's address bar. The bookmark icon looks like a small flag with a star on it. Selecting this icon will display the browser's Bookmarks screen, which shows all of your current bookmarks as page thumbnails (see Figure 11.5). The current page will appear in the top-left corner of the screen with the word Add superimposed on it. Select the page's thumbnail, either type a new name or accept the default, and select OK to add the bookmark.

You can also bookmark a page by pressing the device's Menu button, then Bookmarks, which takes you to the same place as selecting the bookmark icon on the browser's address bar. In addition, you can press the Menu button, then More, then Add bookmark. This will display the same dialog box as before, prompting you to change or confirm the bookmark name. It will not, however, display the Bookmarks screen.

You can navigate back to a bookmarked page by pressing the device's Menu button, then Bookmarks, to display the Bookmarks screen. Simply select any thumbnail to go to that page.

The same Bookmarks screen also includes tabs for Most visited and History. Most visited lists the sites you frequently visit, allowing you to quickly return to your favorite sites even if they are not bookmarked. History displays all of the pages you have visited in the last month.

You can get even quicker access to pages by saving them as shortcuts directly on your

Figure 11.5
The browser's Bookmarks screen, showing the page I want to add in the top-left corner

home screen. While viewing a page, press the phone's Menu button, then More, then Add shortcut to Home.

CHANGE THE HOME PAGE

While Google's search page provides a convenient starting place, you may decide you would prefer a different page as your browser's home page. You can set a bookmarked page by going to the Bookmarks screen on your browser and long-pressing on the desired page's thumbnail, then selecting Set as homepage from the menu that appears.

You can also change the home page by pressing the Menu button, then selecting More, then Settings. Scroll down to the Set home page option and select it, then type the address of the page you wish to use as the home page.

INSTALLING A DIFFERENT BROWSER

While the default browser from Google is very good, you may decide that you wish to experiment with one of the alternate browsers currently available on the Market. While almost all browsers will display web pages in basically the same way, other browsers may offer features not found in the default.

Dolphin

A long-popular alternate browser for Android is Dolphin. If you are running Android 2.0 or later, you can get Dolphin Browser HD from the Market; users running Android older than 2.0 can get a version without the "HD" moniker. Regardless, both are free.

Dolphin browser includes tabs, which is one major feature missing on the default phone browser. As noted earlier, however, the default browser for your tablet already has tabs (see Figure 11.6). Tabbed browsing allows you to open multiple web pages within the same browser window; odds are very good that you have at least seen tabbed browsing before as every major desktop browser has included the feature for several years.

Dolphin also incorporates many more features into the main interface than does the default browser. You can access book-

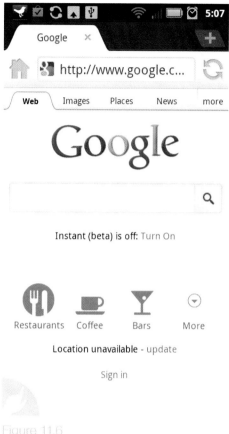

Figure 11.6

The Dolphin browser showing tabs for navigating to multiple websites

marks and your most-visited sites by simply swiping your finger to the right, while swiping to the left reveals a toolbar with an option to browse full screen, hiding both the browser's address and tab bar and the phone's Notifications Bar. In full-screen mde, you can swipe down to reveal a menu screen to switch between open tabs.

Dolphin supports the creation of plug-ins by third-party vendors. You can access a list of plug-ins by selecting the puzzle-piece icon at the bottom of the toolbar, then selecting Get more Add-ons. As of this writing, almost 50 add-ons are available, doing everything from changing how you view web pages to helping protect your passwords. You can also download the plug-ins directly from the Market.

You can also apply themes to the browser to change its overall appearance. Themes are available from the Android Market. Most of the themes simply change the color scheme of the browser to something other than the default green.

Opera

Opera is an old standby in the desktop browser scene. While most casual users have likely never heard of it, many web professionals rely heavily on Opera thanks to the fact that in many environments it displays pages faster than its competitors. Opera offers an Android-based version of its browser, known as Opera Mini, free on the Market (see Figure 11.7).

Like Dolphin, Opera supports tabbed browsing, although it does so through a somewhat unusual interface: Rather than arranging the tabs along the top of the browser like Dolphin and most desktop browsers, Opera bundles the open tabs into a single button in a toolbar at the bottom of the screen, resulting in an experience more like the default browser's multiple windows than a true tabbed browser.

Opera's biggest feature is one which is well hidden but important if you are not on an unlimited data plan. Rather than simply pulling down web pages, the browser relies on compression technology that the company claims can reduce your bandwidth usage by as much as 90 percent.

The browser also includes a feature called Opera Link that allows you to syn-

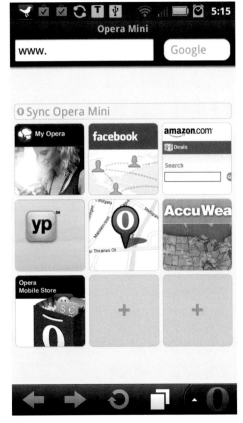

Figure 11.7
The Opera Mini browser

chronize your bookmarks between your device and your desktop computer, as long as you also use the Opera browser on your desktop.

Mozilla Firefox

If you are like me, a fan of Firefox, you can download the Android version from the Market. The browser features many of the same features as Dolphin and Opera, including tabbed browsing and the ability to sync with desktop versions to share bookmarks and open tabs (see Figure 11.8). Like Opera Mini, Firefox presents its tabs in a somewhat strange interface: You access the tabs by swiping to the right, which reveals a sidebar with your tabs. Swiping to the left reveals another sidebar from which you can add and access bookmarks.

DESKTOP BROWSING FROM YOUR DEVICE

Many websites are beginning to recognize that browsing on the smaller form factor of a phone requires a different page design. Some site designers create their pages so that the design seemlessly adapts to your screen, but a lot of sites instead provide

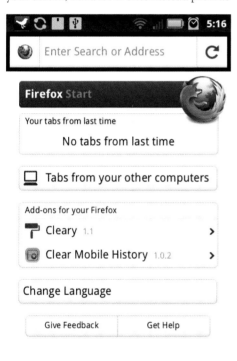

Firefox on Android

a specific, mobile-only version of the pages. Often, these mobile-only sites present different, and unfortunately often less, content then their full-sized versions. Sometimes, the designer is really doing you a favor, as navigating the full-sized version of sites on a small screen can be quite difficult. Other times, however, the sites use the mobile version to do little more than push paid content or their own apps. The mobile version may also be less than ideal on the larger screens available on tablets.

All browsers, whether on mobile devices or the desktop, identify themselves to web servers, and sites use this identifier to redirect users to the mobile version. The default browser in Android provides a hidden but simple way to change this identifier, allowing you to browse the full-sized versions of sites.

Open the default browser and type about:debug. Nothing will appear to happen, but you can now open the browser settings by either pressing the Menu button or, on tablets, the Settings drop-down in the top-right corner. In the Settings screen, you will now see a Debug option (see Figure 11.9). Select that, then choose UAString and select Desktop. Use the Back button to return to the browser, and you will now be able to access the normal versions of most websites.

There are two important caveats to be aware of here. First, some older devices, particularly phones, may not remember this setting the next time the browser opens, so you will have to repeat these steps each time. Second, not all sites use this identifier to present mobile content, so you may still encounter mobile versions on some sites.

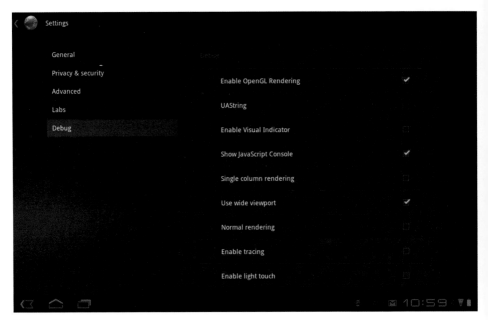

General

Privacy & security

Advanced

Labs

Debug

Debug

Enable OpenGL Rendering

UAString

Enable Visual Indicator

Show JavaScript Console

Single column rendering

Use wide viewport

Normal rendering

Enable tracing

Enable light touch

Figure 11.9

The Debug settings

PART III

Working and Playing

Documents

The Skim

We are still some time away from having our mobile devices completely replace laptop and desktop computers, but we are getting close. I have been using my phone as my primary e-mail and Twitter platform for some time, and I have taken several business trips where I was able to leave my laptop behind and rely solely on my phone and tablet. Only a year ago, when I wrote the first edition of this book, creating new content on a mobile device was still very limited; today, creating many types of documents, including those supported by Microsoft Office, is becoming increasingly possible.

That said, I will not be getting rid of my laptop any time soon. The simple reality is that laptops and desktops remain much more powerful than any mobile device, and a wide variety of software is simply not available. Still, the number of things now possible on my smaller devices still amazes me.

PDF

In the early 1990s, many users consistently encountered difficulties sharing documents with others, as those documents were more than likely in incompatible formats. Workers at a company that used Word-Perfect could not easily exchange information with other workers at companies that relied on Microsoft Word. Adobe created the Portable

Document Format, or PDF, as a solution: While the WordPerfect users could not send an editable document to the Word users, they could at least send one that was readable.

Today, format incompatibility, particularly in office environments using word processors, is much less of a concern, mostly due to the total dominance of the market that Microsoft Word now enjoys. Even still, those few offices (mostly in the legal realm) that use WordPerfect no longer have to worry about incompatibility, because for the most part Word and WordPerfect can now read each other's documents. PDF still has a role to play in those situations, but its primary use today is in protecting documents: The very noneditability that was initially perceived as a drawback to the format is now one of its biggest advantages.

For the most part, you cannot create new documents as PDFs. Rather, the vast majority of users convert existing documents into the format, using a variety of techniques. You can rely on Adobe Acrobat, but a lot of the software you use on your computer may include the ability to convert to PDF without Acrobat. Microsoft Office 2010 on Windows can convert Word, Excel, or PowerPoint documents to PDF without Acrobat. Creative professionals using the other programs in the Adobe Creative Suite, such as Photoshop, Illustrator, and InDesign, can likewise convert to PDF without additional software. Macintosh users have the ability to convert almost any document on their computer to PDF.

Converting to PDF, however, is only half of the equation: You also need to be able to read documents. Most often, reading on desktop and laptop computers is

accomplished via the free Adobe Reader software, although alternate readers do exist. On your Android device, you have the exact same solution: You can read PDFs sent to you thanks to any one of several dozen PDF readers in the Market, including Adobe's official version of Reader (see Figure 12.1).

You will likely get PDFs on your device in one of three ways: by clicking a link on a website, by having one sent as an e-mail attachment, or by manually copying one to your phone's SD card.

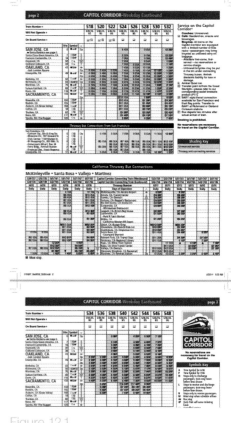

Figure 12.1

Reading a PDF on the phone via the Adobe Reader

WORKING WITH GOOGLE DOCS

Google Docs is a free, web-based alternative to a standard office software suite. It includes a word processor, spreadsheet, presentation, drawing, and form application. All documents you create in Google Docs are saved to their servers, meaning that they can be accessed at any time from any computer — or device — with web access.

In order to start working with Google Docs, you need a Google account, which, of course, you already have. You can create new documents on your computer by going to http://docs.google.com. You will need to log in with your Google username and password, at which point you will be taken to the main Google Docs page. On the left-hand side of the page, you will see a Create new button that presents you with a menu of choices of which kind of document you wish to create. If you select Document, a new tab will open in your browser, allowing you to create a document in Google's word processing application. Although not as fully featured as something like Microsoft Word, the Google application allows you to type your document and apply most of the common formatting you are familiar with, such as changing the font, size, and color of text. You can save your document at any time by clicking the Save now button in the top-right corner of the screen, although the application does automatically save for you every few seconds.

You can return to the main Google docs window by simply switching back to its tab in the browser or by closing the document's tab. Selecting Presentation from the Create new button opens Google's alternative to PowerPoint. As with the word processor, you will find many of the basic features here if you are familiar with PowerPoint. The biggest missing feature — the exclusion of which can be considered either a good or bad thing, depending on your views of PowerPoint — is that you cannot apply animation or transition effects in Google's application. You can right-click on items on the slide and select Incremental Reveal to control how text boxes appear on the slide, but that is as close as the application comes to the sorts of effects with which you may be familiar. When in the Presentation application, you will find a Start presentation and Save button in the top-right corner. As with the word processor, presentations are automatically saved on a regular basis.

The main Google Docs window's Create new button also includes an option to create a new spreadsheet, which opens a window and presents an application similar to Microsoft Excel. While again some more advanced features are missing, the basics are all here, including the most important feature for any spreadsheet application: the ability to simplify math through functions. If you are familiar with editing documents and using functions in Excel, you will find the Google Docs version easy to use.

The Google Doc's drawing program is the one in the set that offers the fewest features. If you need to create some relatively simple drawings to accompany a presentation, it might suit your needs, but artists in particular will find it lacking. It functions much more closely to the embedded drawing tools in Microsoft Office programs than a true drawing application.

Finally, perhaps the most unique of the Google Docs applications is Forms, which allows you to create surveys with a variety of question types. Best of all, it automatically records the responses in a spreadsheet, making it easy to analyze the results.

One of the nicest features of Google Docs is the ability to share documents with others. Any document can be shared with any number of users, and you have the ability to control whether those users can edit or merely view documents. In this way, workers at remote sites can have easy access to important documents; one training center I work for with sites throughout California maintains its master class schedule on Google Docs, allowing the managers at each site to view and edit the schedule for all sites.

All of the Google Docs applications are available on your Android device via the browser by navigating to http://m.google.com/docs, but you will find a limited feature set, including a lack of ability to edit word processing and presentation documents. Fortunately, you have much more functionality by using the Google Docs app, available for free in the Market. As you are already

logged into your Google account on your device, you need not log in when you launch the app. Instead, you will see a dashboard that allows you to access all of your current Docs items or create new documents (see Figure 12.2).

When opening existing documents, you should be able to fully navigate and edit their contents. The app has a few quirks; for example, when you add a row to a spreadsheet, you have to manually refresh from the menu before you will see the new data, but overall it works well.

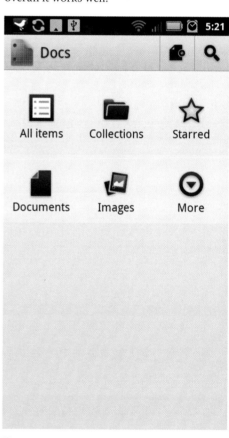

Figure 12.2

The main page of Google Docs, showing the documents I have created

TIDBIT

A few applications exist in the Market to work with Google Docs, but in September 2010 the company announced that it was readying an official application that would allow users to edit and view documents in Google Docs, with the focus on improving security. Unfortunately, the app was not released in time to be included in this book, but may be available in the Market by the time you read this.

You can also create new docs in the app. From the main page, select the icon in the top-right corner that looks like a page with a plus sign. Select the type of document you want to create, give it a name, then begin editing (see Figure 12.3).

WORKING WITH MICROSOFT OFFICE DOCUMENTS

A wide variety of programs exist to allow you to work with Microsoft Office documents on your phone. You should carefully evaluate your needs for an Office application before downloading a free one or purchasing a commercial app. In particular, you should decide if you need merely to be able to read documents, which most of the free apps can accomplish, or whether you need to be able to edit documents, which in general will require that you purchase an app.

One such paid app that not only allows you to both read and edit documents but also allows you to create new ones is Quickoffice. Many devices have Quickoffice preinstalled, but if you do not have it, or if you have the free version (which does not allow for the creation of new documents), you can purchase it from the Market.

Quickoffice can read, edit, and create new Microsoft Word, Excel, and PowerPoint documents, as well as read PDFs. The application even supports documents created in the newest versions of Office.

Editing Documents in Quickoffice

In order to edit documents in Quickoffice, you need first to transfer the file to your device. Perhaps the easiest way to do this is via e-mail; simply attach the document and send or have it sent to an e-mail account that you can access on your device (see Chapter 5 for details on working with e-mail on your device.) When the message arrives, open the attachment, which will either open directly in Quickoffice or, if you have more than one application on your device that can handle documents, you can choose Quickoffice from the dialog box that appears.

You can also attach your device to your computer via USB and drag documents from your hard drive to your SD card. See

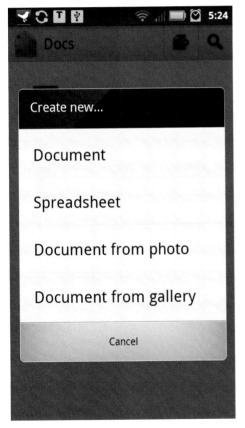

Figure 12.3
A Google spreadsheet displaying on the phone. Select the Edit link to alter data.

Chapter 1 for details. If you choose this method, you will need to open Quickoffice and select Browse from its start-up screen.

It may not be immediately apparent that the document is editable, as Quickoffice does not display any tools, but you can simply tap in the section of the document you wish to edit to place your cursor. Then press the Menu button on your device, choose Keyboard, and begin typing (see Figure 12.4).

You can apply limited formatting to Word documents by pressing the Menu button and selecting Format. Be aware that an

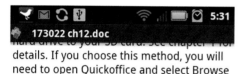

details. If you choose this method, you will need to open Quickoffice and select Browse from its startup screen.

It may not be immediately apparent that the document is editable, as Quickoffice does not display any tools, but you can simply choose in the section of the document you wish to edit to place your cursor. Then, press the Menu button on your phone, choose Keyboard, and begin typing (see Figure 12.4).

You can apply limited formatting to Word documents by pressing the Menu button

Figure 12.4

Editing a Microsoft Word document in Quickoffice

important limitation of the program is that it does not contain an undo function, so if you make a mistake in editing the document, you will either need to manually fix the mistake or close the document without saving changes.

Excel documents function in much the same manner: Either transfer the document to your SD card manually or e-mail it, then open it in Quickoffice. You can double-tap a cell to select it and then type values into the box at the top; unlike with the Word app, the keyboard will automatically appear. Pressing the Menu button gives you access to options to set the number format or switch to other worksheets in the document. You can change the text formatting by pressing Menu, then More, then Font Format. The program supports a full range of Excel's functions, but they must be typed manually into a cell.

PowerPoint documents can be opened in Quickoffice. Initially, you will see thumbnails of each slide (see Figure 12.5). You can double-tap the slide to zoom in or out, and use the Menu button to switch to a slide show view. The text on the slides can be edited by long-pressing the text you wish to edit and selecting Edit Text. You can only change the text itself; formatting either the text or the slides is not possible.

Creating New Documents

You can create new documents for Word, Excel, and PowerPoint in Quickoffice (see Figure 12.6). Keep in mind, however, that entering text on a device, even with Swype, is not as quick or easy — or accurate — as typing on a traditional keyboard, so this capability is unlikely to persuade you to dump your laptop in favor of your device.

Figure 12.5
A PowerPoint presentation open in Quickoffice

Figure 12.6
A new document created in Quickoffice.

You can create new documents for Word and Excel in Quickoffice (see Figure 12-6). Keep in mind, however, that entering text on a device, even with Swype, is not as quick or easy @@md or accurate @@md as typing on a traditional keyboard, so this capability is unlikely to convince you to dump your laptop in favor of your device!

When you create new documents, you are first prompted to select the type. Unfortunately, Quickoffice is not as clear here as it could be, as your choices are Word Document and Word 97–2003 Document. The app presents a similarly vague set of choices for Excel and PowerPoint. What it is really asking is if you want the document to be created using Microsoft's newer file formats — .docx for Word, .xlsx for Excel, and .pptx for PowerPoint — or whether you would prefer to use the older formats. The new formats create docu-ments that can only be opened and edited by Office 2007 and 2010, so if you are still using an older version of Office or if you need to exchange the documents with people who are, you should select the older format.

Other Applications

Quickoffice is not the only app in the Market designed to work with Microsoft Office documents. Another popular appli-cation is Documents to Go, which offers a free version for viewing Word and Excel documents, or a paid version that adds

PowerPoint and PDF viewing along with editing capabilities.

READING E-BOOKS

Reading books in digital formats is either the best thing to happen to literature since Guttenberg, or the worst. As a devoted reader, I resisted serious reading on devices for a long time. That changed shortly after I purchased a Nook Color, however. While

TIP

It is actually possible to work around the limitation of only being able to read books you have downloaded from Amazon, but it takes some work. Obviously, you should not take this as a license to download books illegally, but there are nonetheless times when you may have a book you acquired legitimately through another source. For example, as the author of the *Adobe Flash Catalyst CS5 Bible*, I was able to get an electronic copy of it directly from the publisher, but as I had not downloaded it from Amazon, the Kindle app was not willing to open it. After doing some digging online, I discovered that the app, quite obviously, only syncs with Amazon's server when it is online. Therefore, you can copy a book you did not download into the Kindle's directory, then turn off both Wi-Fi and 3G, launch the app and read the book successfully. The easiest way to disable Wi-Fi and 3G, by the way, is to turn on Airplane mode. You just need to be sure to move the book's file back out of the Kindle's directory before you go back online.

I still love my local bookstore, my Nook is now a constant companion.

As with the mobile market itself, the e-book market is for the time being divided into a variety of formats. Thus, you may need several apps on your phone.

One of the more common formats is PDF, which as you have already seen can be read using the official Adobe Reader app or any of the other PDF apps available in the Market. Most likely, you will need to transfer the PDF to your device by manually copying it to the SD card or via e-mail, although you may also be able to download it directly from a website.

Amazon Kindle

Another very common format is that used by the Amazon Kindle. While the company primarily advertises the Kindle as a stand-alone device, it has also created a Kindle app to allow you to purchase and read e-books directly on your phone. The official Amazon Kindle app is preloaded on many devices, but if you do not have it you can download it free from the Market.

You can only read books that you have downloaded from Amazon's website on the app. The company stores your purchase and download history both in the app and on its website, and every time you launch it, the app compares the books in its library to those recorded online. Unfortunately, the app's response to finding books it does not recognize is not exactly ideal: It simply crashes, and will not start up again until the offending book is removed.

In order to download books that the app will accept, open the app, press the phone's Menu button, and select Kindle Store. This will launch your browser and display the store, which is organized into categories including best-sellers, new titles, and classics (see Figure 12.7). You can browse by category or search for specific titles.

While most books being published today are available electronically, many older titles have also been converted, and a lot of those are available free of charge. The Kindle Store's main page includes a link to free popular classics, with great works such as Sir Arthur Conan Doyle's *The Adventures of Sherlock Holmes*, Bram Stoker's *Dracula*, most of the works of Shakespeare, and my

own personal favorite book, Mary Shelley's *Frankenstein* (see Figure 12.8).

Newer releases almost always cost nearly as much as the print version. Keep in mind that the majority of the cost involved in producing a book is in paying authors and editors and in real labor costs such as layout, and not the actual printing, so you should not expect switching to reading titles electronically to significantly reduce

Figure 12.7

Categories of e-books available in the Kindle Store

Letter 1

TO Mrs. Saville, England

St. Petersburgh, Dec. 11th, 17--

You will rejoice to hear that no disaster has accompanied the commencement of an enterprise which you have regarded with such evil forebodings. I arrived here yesterday, and my first task is to assure my dear sister of my welfare and increasing confidence in the success of my undertaking.

I am already far north of London, and as I walk in the streets of Petersburgh, I feel a cold northern breeze play upon my cheeks, which braces my

Figure 12.8

Mary Shelley's *Frankenstein*. If you think you know the story from all of the bad movies that have been supposedly based on it, do yourself a favor and read the actual novel.

your book-buying budget. All books you purchase with the Kindle app are processed through Amazon, so if you already have an account you can sign into it on your phone and use the one-click ordering process, which enables you to begin reading a book within a few seconds of deciding to buy it. If you do not have an account already, you can follow the steps outlined in the Kindle Store to create one.

While reading a book, you can simply swipe your finger from the right to the left to "turn" the page. You can also press the phone's Menu button and choose View Options to adjust the font size and background color. The app will automatically remember your spot in the book, although you can manually add bookmarks as you go if you need the ability to return to multiple spots later.

Aldiko

A popular, free e-book reader for Android is Aldiko. The app comes with Sun Tzu's *Art of War* and H.G. Wells' *The Invisible Man* preinstalled, and includes the ability to download free public domain books as well as free books from a few other sources (see Figure 12.9). Aldiko only supports books in the ePub format.

Aldiko's only real limitation is that it cannot download books from commercial sites such as Amazon, so you will not be able to read the latest best-sellers. However, if you are more into the classics and lesser-known authors, you will likely not mind the app's selections.

Reading on Aldiko is almost identical to the Kindle app; in fact, if you were just shown a book in both, you would be unlikely to tell the difference (see Figure 12.10).

Nook

The Barnes & Noble Nook is an Android-based dedicated eReader, designed to compete with Amazon's Kindle. The newer Nook Color is based on Android (FroYo, to be specific), and offers a web browser and apps, but it is still mainly an eReader.

Like Amazon, Barnes & Noble also has a free Nook app available in the Android Market. The Nook app offers access to the Nook store, from which you can purchase books from Barnes & Noble. It also syncs with your Nook account, so you can access

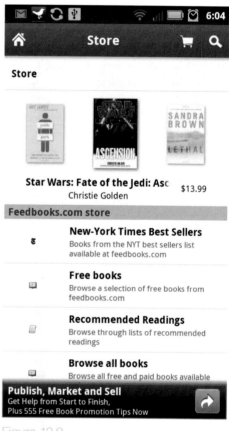

Figure 12.9

The Store page in Aldiko

any books you have purchased for your physical Nook on your phone or tablet. In fact, you can begin reading a book on the actual Nook, then open the book on your phone and tablet and be taken to the spot you left off on the Nook. If you continue reading in Android, your Nook will update and take you to the correct spot when you return to that device. Note that this synchronization only works if your Nook is connected to a Wi-Fi signal when you read.

Buying Books from Google

You can now also buy books directly from the Android Market on your device. The books offered by Google are in the ePub format, so you can read them in Aldiko or the Nook app, but not the Kindle app. The big advantage of buying via the Market is that Google already has all of your account information, so it is much more effortless than most other options.

THE TRAIL OF THE MEAT

Dark spruce forest frowned on either side the frozen waterway. The trees had been stripped by a recent wind of their white covering of frost, and they seemed to lean towards each other, black and ominous, in the fading light. A vast silence reigned over the land. The land itself was a desolation, lifeless, without movement, so lone and cold that the spirit of it was not even that of sadness. There was a hint in it of laughter, but of a laughter more terrible than any sadness— a laughter that was mirthless as the smile of the sphinx, a laughter cold as the frost and partaking of the grimness of infallibility. It was the masterful and

Figure 12.10

Reading a book in Aldiko

Games

The Skim

recently heard someone describe smartphones as a technology that allows users to kill time productively, and thought it an apt description of how I actually use my phone a lot of the time. I will pull it out to quickly check Twitter or e-mail while I am in line at the store or waiting to board a plane. That said, I have to admit that while I use my phone a lot to kill time, it is not always all that productive: There are plenty of times that I will spend time in line playing a game rather than checking e-mail.

The good news for Android users is that the variety of games available on the platform will suit almost any taste. Serious gamers can find games that might rival some found on desktop computers, while more casual gamers like myself can find titles — usually for free — to match our tastes as well.

PUZZLE GAMES

If you are looking for casual games that you can play in short bursts here and there that will nonetheless require at least some thinking, the Market offers a large selection of puzzle games.

Andoku

I have an affinity to Sudoku. It is something that you can do a little at a time, and can definitely be challenging. When I got my first Android phone, Sudoku apps were among the first I looked for. I tried out a variety of the free apps on the Market, and by far the best I came across was Andoku (see Figure 13.1). It provides puzzles in five levels ranging from "easy" to "fiendish," with 100 puzzles in each level. All puzzles are timed, and the app keeps track of your fastest and slowest times as well as your average, so you can see if you are somehow managing to get better with each game. The nicest thing about Andoku, however, and what really set it apart from the other Soduko games on the Market was its intelligent input. Too many others relied on the phone's keyboard, which often makes entering numbers slow, while Andoku presents a number pad at the bottom of the screen. Also, it is not ad supported, so you will not find yourself constantly interrupting your game when you accidentally click an ad.

Rush Hour

Years ago, I was given the board game Rush Hour for Christmas. Rush Hour is a simple puzzle game where you take a set of plastic cars and move them around on a board. The goal is to move enough cars out of the way to "free" your car to exit the board. Now, I no longer need to pull out the physical game to play, as Rush Hour is available for Android in both a free and a paid version (see Figure 13.2). The object is the same: You play the red car and need to move the other cars, trucks, and occasional limousine out of the way so that you can get to the exit. The game seems almost silly when described, but I think most people will find it fairly addictive. The game has four difficulty levels. The free version contains 10 puzzles per level, while the paid version has an astounding 650 puzzles per level.

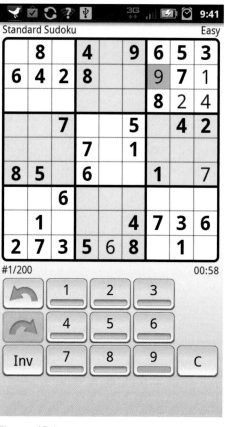

Figure 13.1

Andoku, an excellent Sudoku game

My only objection to the game is that it does not have a tablet version. You can install the phone version on a tablet without difficulty, but you will be playing on a small board in the middle of the screen rather than something full-sized.

Peggle

Peggle has been around since 2007 on desktop computers and game consoles, but I first discovered it when it appeared as an Amazon Free App of the Day, and I got hooked pretty quickly. I am lucky I got it free, but it is in my opinion well worth the

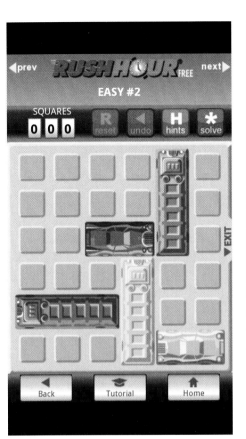

Figure 13.2
Rush Hour Free

and scoring at least 350,000 points. Along the way, you are helped by a group of Peggle Masters — characters that provide you with additional powers when you hit one of two randomly positioned green pegs.

Chuzzle

Chuzzle, another highly addictive puzzle game from PopCap, follows the pattern of a plethora of similar games: you have a grid of different colored objects that you can rearrange. Whenever you get three or more of the same color aligned, they disappear, clearing room for more.

What sets Chuzzle apart from all of the other games is that instead of gems or blocks or whatever, you get a set of rather cute, fuzzy characters — the Chuzzles — which sort of resemble multicolored Tribbles (see Figure 13.4). The game is also a bit more challenging than a lot of the other titles, as the Chuzzles will lock if you get too many groups of three, and you sometimes get giant Chuzzles popping up on the screen for an added challenge.

$2.99. Note that as of this writing, Peggle is only available via the Amazon Appstore, and not in the Android Market.

The game play is pretty straight-forward: You launch a series of balls from the top of the screen through an arrangement of 100 pegs (see Figure 13.3). Each peg your ball hits will vanish, allowing you to gradually clear the board. The official goal of the game is to clear the 25 randomly placed orange pegs on each level, but once you have finished that on all 55 levels, you can go back through and try for two additional challenges on each level: clearing all 100 pegs

Figure 13.3
One of the many levels of Peggle

CLASSIC BOARD GAMES

Google groups quite a few games under its "Brain and Puzzle" category that I would more accurately classify as board games, including classics such as chess, checkers, backgammon, and mancala.

Chess for Android

While the exact origins of chess are deeply debated, no one questions that people have been playing the game, or at least something similar, for something close to 1500 years. From fairly early on, people have attempted to create computer-based chess games that can provide fun yet challenging game play; in 1997, a computer known as Deep Blue became the first machine to defeat a World Chess Champion when it beat Garry Kasparov. It is no surprise then that the Market is full of chess games, but one of the nicest is titled simply Chess for Android (see Figure 13.5). The app presents

a classic, easy-to-view board. It highlights the spots to which each piece can move and displays the game's history on the lower portion of the screen. I discovered that not only is the app a great way to play chess, it is also a good learning tool, as I have been using it to help teach the game to my daughter. It contains eight levels, although these seem to relate more to the speed with which your opponent moves than the actual skill of the opponent.

Checkers for Android

I will admit that I've never been the biggest fan of checkers. I know that there is actually a lot of strategy to the game, and perhaps I just have not devoted enough effort to learning it, so it is still in the range of games I can play somewhat mindlessly. That, of course, means that I can pretty much count on getting beaten every time by my phone's Checkers for Android, made

Figure 13.4
The Chuzzles

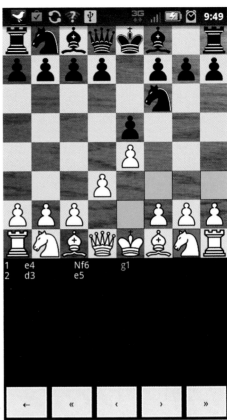

Figure 13.5
Chess for Android

by the same developer as Chess for Android (see Figure 13.6). But the look and feel of the checkers app are very similar to the chess app, including the same levels option that merely slows down the opponent. A much prettier version of Checkers, made by AI Factory Ltd, is also available for $1.99, but gameplay is essentially the same, as it is after all checkers.

Backgammon

Backgammon is another classic game that has survived for centuries, with sets for a very similar game having been discovered

in Iran dating to 3000 BCE. Like chess and checkers, dozens of backgammon games exist on the Market, and the free game simply titled Backgammon Free by AI Factory is among the best (see Figure 13.7). It contains a very nice, classic-looking board and sound effects of die rolling on wood. One of its more interesting features, however, is an anticheating mode. Backgammon games rely partially on luck, thanks to the roll of the dice, but also on skill, and skillful players can make moves that increase their chances of being able to capitalize on good rolls while minimizing their opponent's opportuni-

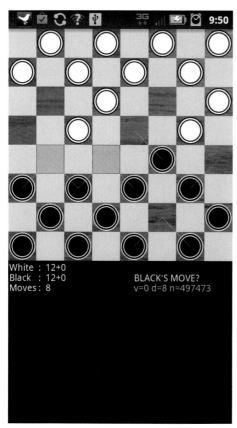

White : 12+0
Black : 12+0   BLACK'S MOVE?
Moves: 8   v=0 d=8 n=497473

Figure 13.6
Checkers for Android

ties. Thus, it can often appear as though the computer is cheating by getting better rolls. To prove that this is not the case, the game actually includes an option that allows the human player to roll an actual set of physical dice and input the values, thus bypassing the game's die rolls and proving that you keep losing simply because the game is better than you. A paid version is available for $1.99 that removes the ads at the top of the screen.

Mancala

Mancala is not technically a game, but rather a category of games. However, the term has come to be commonly associated with the game Kalah, and the two terms are often used interchangeably, particularly on the Market. The game has its origins in agricultural societies, so many games use the analogy of moving seeds from one pocket to the next, but most modern versions of the game, including the ones you will find in the Market, use instead the idea of moving gem stones. To play, you take all of the stones out of one pocket and place them, one at a time, into the adjacent pockets. You can capture your opponent's stones by counting correctly and ending your turn in an empty pocket. The game ends when all of the pockets from one side of the board are empty. The free app in the Market simply called Mancala by Xoise Solutions is among the nicest available (see Figure 13.8).

ACTION GAMES

When many people think of video games, they think lots of action and loud explosions. If that is your style, you will find plenty of choices on Android. Unfortunately, few of these games are free.

RoboDefense

Tower defense games are almost a genre by themselves. These games revolve around the idea of you defending some kind of territory by placing weapons in the path of a seemingly never-ending horde of attackers. You are not responsible for actually shooting your opponents; instead, your guns or other weapons fire by themselves, leaving you to figure out the best placement for your defenses. All of the games provide you with limited resources and defense of varying quality — and cost. While a lot of tower defense games exist on the market, one of the more entertaining is Robo-Defense (see Figure 13.9). The graphics are a bit too small to make out details, but the idea is that you have to place guns in the path of robots who are attacking what

LISTEN to a BEST SELLER Today!!!
Ads by AdMob
audible.com

You 167   Cpu (1) 161

64

Undo

Figure 13.7
Backgammon

TIP

The only real challenge in finding games to play on your Android device is in trying to choose which ones to download, as the Market is full of thousands of titles in practically every genre. The Market lists games in four basic categories: Arcade & Action, Brain & Puzzle, Cards & Casino, and Casual. Unfortunately, you will quickly come across the Market's biggest limitation: It is designed around the idea of searching for apps, not browsing for them, so once you go into any of these categories you find an overwhelming list of titles, which are presented in a seemingly random order. You could thus spend all of your time browsing for games rather than actually playing them. You might get lucky and stumble upon a couple here and there, but you are unfortunately better off just doing what Google wants you to do in the first place, which is search. Do not search for specific titles, unless, of course, you know the exact one for which you are looking, but instead search on more general subjects, such as Sudoku or hearts or poker. This will generally result in a good list of the titles available for that type of game, which will allow you to find one you like. When evaluating games, I would definitely recommend that you also look at the comments to see what others thought of the title.

appears to be some sort of fortress. Lower levels tend to be fairly easy, but higher levels become quite difficult. The game is avail- able in a free version with limited maps and levels and a larger, more expansive paid version.

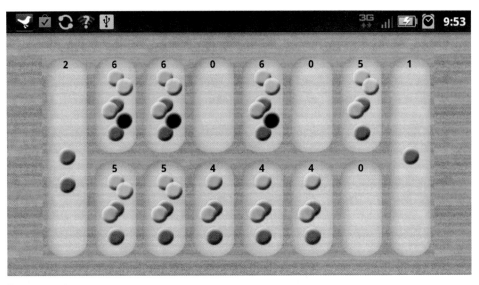

Figure 13.8
Mancala

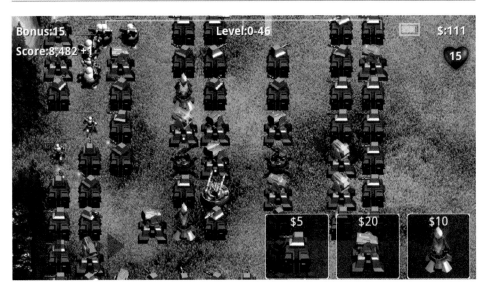

Figure 13.9
RoboDefense

Plants vs. Zombies

A slightly different, and in many ways more entertaining, twist in the tower defense genre is Plants vs. Zombies (see Figure 13.10). Long one of the most popular titles on iPhones, Plants vs. Zombies is now available for Android, but only through the Amazon Appstore. It is well worth the $2.99.

The idea is the same as any tower defense: You place weapons in the path of oncoming hordes of enemies in an attempt to stop them from reaching their goal. In this version, however, your weapons are a variety of plants, the oncoming hordes are the undead, and the tower is your house. Exactly why plants are able to defeat zombies is not fully explored, but not terribly important either.

Angry Birds

On paper, Angry Birds seems like quite a silly game. The story, such as it is, revolves around a group of pigs who have stolen the eggs from a bunch of birds. The pigs have then fortified themselves inside rather poorly made structures of wood, stone, and ice, and the birds have decided to hurl themselves at the structures in order to kill the pigs. Or something. In the game, you take the role of the birds — in each level, you pull back a slingshot and toss birds at the pigs' structures, which then collapse down on them (see Figure 13.11). You have a limited number of birds, and the object is to kill all of the pigs in as few shots as possible. It is unquestionably silly, but also shockingly addictive. Angry Birds is one of the most popular games in the mobile space and has turned into something of a cultural phenomenon. The game has been referenced in movies and TV shows, while software giant Electronic Arts recently paid $40 million for Rovio, the company behind the game. Stores

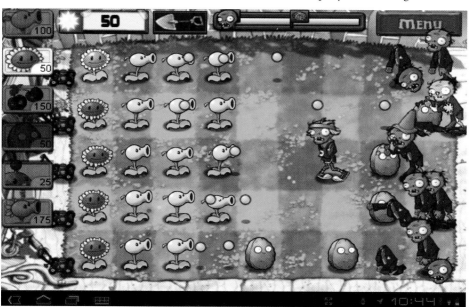

Figure 13.10
Plants vs. Zombies

Figure 13.11
Angry Birds

are now filled with Angry Birds merchandise, including everything from T-shirts to the giant stuffed pig my son got me for my birthday this year.

There are two additional versions of the game available: Angry Birds Rio, a tie-in to an animated movie (the game is much better), and Angry Birds Seasons, which has levels themed for Halloween, Christmas, Easter, Valentine's Day, St. Patrick's Day, summer, and the Moon Festival.

CARD GAMES

Card games are some of the most popular electronic games. From solitaire to hearts to Texas Hold'em poker, you will find plenty of options to keep you entertained if you like playing cards.

Solitaire

Many solitaire games exist on the Market, including Klondike Solitaire. The game is as straight-forward as it gets: just the basic

solitaire game. The game includes a variety of options, including the ability to customize both the fronts and backs of the cards and the table. It is ad supported (see Figure 13.12).

Another popular solitaire app is Fun Towers, which essentially reverses the traditional solitaire game, forcing you to pull cards from the stack back into your hand. It is both simple and surprisingly addictive.

Poker

Poker, particularly the Texas Hold'em variety, has become one of the most popular games over the last few years, with ESPN even televising the annual World Series tournament and a plethora of online gaming sites, so it should come as no surprise to see many Android poker apps available. The problem with poker as a video game, however, is that it is very difficult to do well against a computer, because it is a game in which the best hand does not always win thanks to the ability of players

Figure 13.12
Solitaire

While the majority of games for Android are games that have existed in other forms and have merely been ported to the phone, a growing number take advantage of the unique properties of your device.

to bluff, something that computers cannot easily do nor fall victim to. A few apps exist to solve this problem by allowing you to play live, online against other users. One such app is the Red Poker Club, which can be downloaded for free. You are given a set amount of virtual chips with which to play each day. As with other online poker games, you will find a wide variety of players to match up against.

GAMES THAT TAKE ADVANTAGE OF YOUR PHONE'S ABILITIES

While the majority of games for Android are games that have existed in other forms and have merely been ported to the phone, a growing number take advantage of the unique properties of your device.

Abduction!

In Abduction! 2, your object is simple: Help a cow jump up a series of obstacles

to rescue its friends from alien abduction (see Figure 13.13). What makes the game unique is that you control the cow using your device's accelerometer, so if you need it to move to the left to catch a platform, you tilt your device that way. This is also what makes the game fairly hard.

SpecTrek

SpecTrek is an augmented reality ghost-hunting game. The idea is that you use your phone's GPS system to hunt down ghosts in your neighborhood; when you get close to one, you can tilt your phone up and begin using the camera, which overlays the ghost against the real-world backdrop. You can then choose a net icon on the screen to "capture" the ghost.

The game begins with a warning to play it only on foot, as you will obviously be looking at your phone's screen most of the time, rather than paying attention to what is around you, so operating a vehicle of any kind can be dangerous. You should also be aware that playing the game in a crowded environment such as a city can be equally hazardous, not to mention that you're sure to get some odd looks from passers-by. A nice open park is probably the ideal place to play.

CLASSIC GAMES

While the majority of the video games I grew up on are still missing from modern platforms, a few have started to make their way onto my mobile devices. Few if any of these games are free.

Pac-Man

First introduced on May 22, 1980, Pac-Man is without a doubt one of the most famous video games of all time. While many rip-offs of the game exist, its original creator Namco has released an official version that is an exact clone of the arcade classic, complete with the original sound effects (see Figure 13-14). It is one of the very few games I play with the sound on. While expensive by mobile game standards at $4.99, if you are a fan of the game you will need to buy this one. For those fans of the sequel, Ms. Pac-Man is also available, and likewise runs $4.99.

Figure 13.13
Abduction! 2

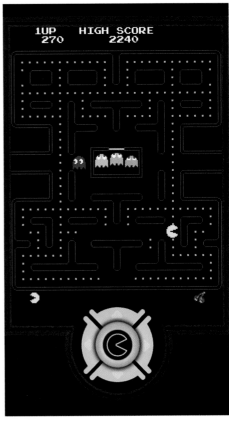

Figure 13.14
The classic Pac-Man

Frogger

I was always a big fan of Frogger. For those who might have grown up after the 1980s, the gameplay in Frogger is pretty simple: Help a frog cross a busy street and strangely busy river to get to its lily pad. The challenge is that our poor amphibian needs to first dodge a series of fast-moving cars and trucks, and then has to cross the river by leaping on logs and turtles while avoiding evil red frogs. The game does not explain why the frog cannot simply swim across the river, but I guess we are not supposed to ask those kinds of questions.

The Android version was developed by Konami, the company behind the original arcade version. While it retains the gameplay of the original, it has somewhat unfortunately been updated with new graphics and an annoying new soundtrack (see Figure 13.15). Despite that, fans of the original should enjoy this update. The game costs $1.99.

Guitar Hero 5

While not nearly as old as Pac-Man and Frogger, Guitar Hero 5 is likely better known to younger audiences. The original

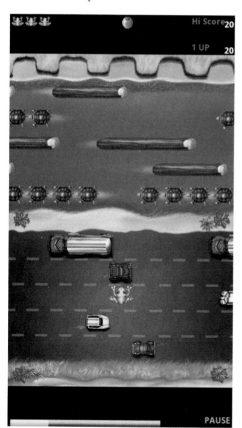

Figure 13.15
Frogger

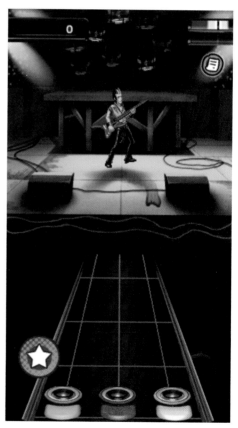

Figure 13.16
Guitar Hero on Android

game, released initially for Sony's Playstation 2 platform but subsequently developed for Xbox and Wii, relied on a custom guitar-shaped controller. The official Android version, for obvious reasons, does not use a special controller, but the gameplay is nonetheless similar to the original, allowing to you "play" along with a song (see Figure 13.16). Tapping on the screen causes the game to lose a lot of its charm, but it can nonetheless be an enjoyable enough way to kill a bit of free time, although it is only available through the Amazon Appstore and runs an expensive $7.99.

WEB-BASED GAMES

Most games available on the web require Flash Player, and because Flash is supported on an ever-increasing percentage of Android devices, most all Android users have the ability to play almost any game you can find online. The only caveat to be aware of is that some sites might detect that you are on a mobile device and block you, although see Chapter 11 for suggestions of how you might get around this.

All you need to do to play Flash-based games on the web is to simply go to the site in question and play as normal (see Figure 13.17). Be aware, however, that while Flash Player has been optimized for mobile, many sites might not be. If a game requires keyboard input, for example, and your phone only has a virtual keyboard, you may find that the keyboard takes up enough space on your screen that the game becomes all but unplayable. Other games may have problems with simply being too large.

Figure 13.17

Playing a Flash-based game at Orisinal.com

192

Other Cool Apps

The Skim

Stargazing with Google Sky Maps ◦ Finding Local Businesses ◦ Getting Movie
and TV Information with IMDb ◦ Creating Shopping Lists ◦ Calculating Tips
◦ Taking Notes with Evernote ◦ Planning Trips with Kayak ◦ Keeping Track of
the Weather with WeatherBug ◦ Researching with Wapedia and Wikimobile ◦
Finding Recipes ◦ Following Your Favorite Sports Teams ◦ Scanning Barcodes ◦
Translating with Google Translate

What separates mobile devices from regular cell phones, of course, are the apps. Apps are what people want to see when you show them your device; they are what device manufacturers focus on in advertising their products; they are how people are making money in the mobile world. Spend enough time browsing the Market and you are likely to find that there is, in fact, an app for that. What "that" is, exactly, depends on your personal taste.

STARGAZING WITH GOOGLE SKY MAPS

From a very early age, I have been fascinated with the stars and space. Some of my earliest memories, in fact, are of hanging outside with my dad, staring up at the stars. As I got older, I began learning about constellations and the science of astronomy. When Halley's Comet last visited Earth in 1986, my parents bought me a telescope, and I can recall spending many evenings outside looking at the planets and stars. Of course, while all of those years of study gave me a better-than-working knowledge of the sky, I still had to rely on paper and plastic star charts to figure out where things were; many times, it was only when I pointed my telescope at a planet that I figured out which one it was.

Now that I have kids, I have the chance to begin to pass on this obsession to them. We still look through that same telescope I had when I was younger, but gone are the plastic circular star charts. Instead, I keep my device with me outside, and when I want to figure out what planet is hanging near the moon or find a particular star, I simply open up Google Sky Maps.

Sky Maps was one of the first apps I downloaded on my old G1; in fact, it was one of my main motivations to get an Android-based smartphone in the first place. Sky Maps is exactly what it says it is. When you launch it, the app uses GPS or, failing that, triangulation from cell towers to determine where you are, and then presents a map of the sky at that moment (see Figure 14.1). You

can identify celestial objects by holding your device above your head and pointing it at the area of the sky you are looking it.

Sky Maps has a lot of options that allow you to configure what you see. You can simply select the screen to view a menu that allows you to turn on or off sets of objects, including stars, constellations, Messier objects, planets, the Right Ascension and Declination grid, and the horizon.

Selecting the screen also gives you the ability to zoom in and out on the map, and the option to switch between manual and automatic modes. Automatic mode has the map display the objects that the device points at, while manual mode lets you move around the sky yourself, regardless of the orientation of the device.

You can also press the Menu button to display still more options. Search lets you find a particular object by name or designation. The search will then display a large

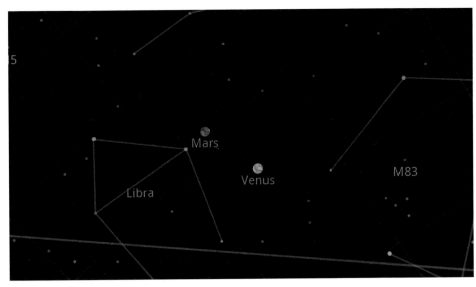

Figure 14.1

Google Sky Maps, showing the current locations of Mars and Venus

circle and an arrow; the circle gradually changes color as you move closer to the object, going from blue when you are looking in completely the wrong direction to red and eventually an expanded yellow circle when you find the object. The menu also allows you to toggle on Night mode, which makes the background black and everything on the display red. Night mode works because your pupils do not expand when exposed to red light, so you can look at the screen and not lose your night vision.

The Gallery displays a selection of pictures of objects taken by the Hubble Space Telescope. You can select any image to view it full screen, and then select Find in sky to be taken back to the map and shown the location of the object to see it yourself (see Figure 14.2). Time Travel lets you see the sky as it will or did appear at any time past or present. So, if you have always been curious about where the moon was on the night of July 20, 1969 (if I have to explain the significance of that date, then I can assume you are not curious about where the moon was), or on your birthday, you can do that. Once you jump to a date, you can use the controls at the top of the screen to begin moving forward or back from that date.

FINDING LOCAL BUSINESSES

The rise of e-commerce over the last two decades has had an undeniably negative impact on smaller local businesses. What used to require a trip to the local independent bookstore or music shop can now be done in the comfort of your own home. Just as important, the web was not much help for local businesses because

> **TIDBIT**
>
> Charles Messier was a seventeenth-century French astronomer who created a catalog of galaxies, nebulae, and star clusters. Today, these objects are known, appropriately, as Messier objects. The objects are known by a numeric designation Messier gave them; for example, the Andromeda galaxy is M31. There are a total of 110 Messier objects. Nineteenth- and twentieth-century astronomers compiled a much longer list, known as the New General Catalogue or NGC, that includes all of the Messier objects, along with about 7700 additional ones, but most professional and amateur astronomers, not to mention Sky Maps, still use the Messier designations for those in his catalog. One of the things that makes the Messier objects compelling is that Messier himself did not have a very powerful telescope, so all of this objects can be seen with either the naked eye or a relatively small, 4-inch telescope.

finding information on the web required that users be at home in front of their computers.

The rise of mobile devices, however, holds the promise to reverse those losses. Now, you can realistically be out with friends and find a good local wine merchant, or track down a hard-to-find rare book that a local used shop happens to carry. Of course, the easiest way to do this is simply use your device's browser to search just as you would normally, or even

Orion Nebula

Back to gallery   Find in sky

Figure 14.2

The Orion Nebula in the Sky Map
Hubble Gallery

start directly from the home screen with
the integrated search.

For certain items, a traditional search will
work well, but for many others it will not.
Unless you live in a very small rural area, a
search for local restaurants is not likely to
be terribly helpful, as you will simply get too
many results. If you are in a large city, even
narrowing down that search by the type of
food you want to eat will still likely give you
too many hits.

Thankfully, several apps exist on the Market to help you narrow things down. Two

popular ones are Where and Yelp. Best of
all, both are free.

WHERE

WHERE is a local directory designed to get
you to local business quickly. When you start
the app, it will determine your location based
on your cell provider's network, which is
generally less accurate than GPS, but in this
case being a block or two off really does not
matter. The app's main page displays a set of
categories. From here, you can access lists of
places to eat, things to do, and special offers.

One of WHERE'S most useful lists is Restaurants (see Figure 14.3). This displays a list
of nearby restaurants, but by selecting the
Filter button at the top of the screen I can
see restaurants organized by type of cuisine,
so it lets me know, for example, that there
are unfortunately no Cuban restaurants
near me, but more pizza places than you can
imagine (the city I live in is known for having an unusually high concentration of pizza
restaurants, for reasons no one can quite
determine). You can select a restaurant
from any of the categories to view its details.
From here, you can select Map to display
the restaurant's location, or choose its
phone number to call for more information
or, if necessary, make reservations.

The app's main screen includes a small
menu along the bottom. The more button
displays a list of additional categories to
search in WHERE, including useful information like weather and coupons.

Another great feature of the application is
its ability to look up nearby gas prices. You
can select the grade of fuel you prefer, and
the app will display gas stations within 10
miles that carry that type of gas and how
much they currently charge, letting you

know that you can save 10 cents a gallon by driving an extra mile.

Yelp

Yelp serves much the same purpose as WHERE by providing a localized directory of businesses and services. If you select the Nearby icon, then one of the categories such as restaurants, you will see that it has about as much information as WHERE (see Figure 14.4). Like Where, Yelp relies heavily on user reviews, and displays star ratings on initial listings and detailed reviews on business pages.

Yelp has less time-sensitive information; for example, it does not display current gas prices or events, but in general has more in-depth business directories. It also allows you to filter the lists based on price or, a particularly nice feature, by businesses that are currently open.

It also has one very cool feature WHERE lacks: the so-called Monocle view. Select this from the main Yelp page, give it a moment to determine your location, and then hold your phone in front of you to see a listing of the restaurants in that direction, displayed on an overlay of your phone's camera view.

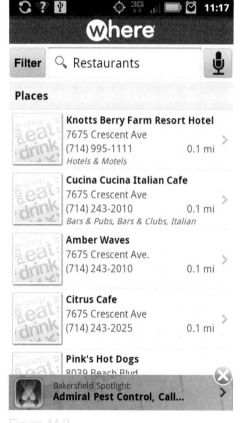

Figure 14.3
The Where Places categories

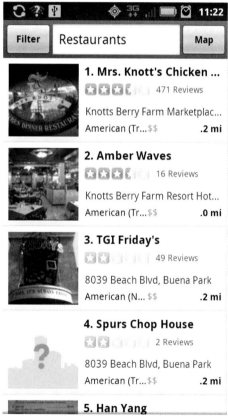

Figure 14.4
Yelp's local restaurant view

GETTING MOVIE AND TV INFORMATION WITH IMDB

As I mentioned earlier, I am a very big movie buff. Many years ago, I actually got into web design because I wanted to build a film review website. As I began working on the site, I needed a quick way to look up details on the movie, such as the names of the director or stars. I do not recall exactly how I discovered the Internet Movie Database, or IMDb, but it quickly became my go-to site for details. It is without question the only site I have continued to visit regularly for the entire time I have been using the web.

IMDb was created off of a collection of lists on a Usenet discussion board about movies. Over time, the list grew to the point that it became impractical to merely view it, and on October 17, 1990, one of the people maintaining the list, Col Needham, released a set of scripts that could be used to search the list. By general agreement, this date is considered the birth of the IMDb. In 1992, it became one of the earliest websites. The organizers incorporated in 1996, and in 1998 the company was purchased by Amazon, which continues to operate it as a private subsidiary. Today, IMDb is one of the most-visited sites on the web and contains information on practically every movie or TV show ever produced.

In 2010, IMDb launched its app for Android, which gives users an easy way to access all of the data on the site. I still use it primarily for the same thing I have always used the site for: to quickly look up the names of people in movies and TV shows I am watching. It is particularly helpful to find the name of that actor in the show you are viewing who you recognize but cannot quite place. You can search the app by pressing the phone's Menu button and selecting Search, or more directly by pressing the phone's Search button.

A key difference between the website and mobile app, however, is that the app also displays local movie times. From the app's main page, simply select US Showtimes to see a list of the movies currently playing in a theater near you. Each movie lists its running time and the local theaters in which it is playing (see Figure 14.5). Select the film's title to go to the IMDb page about the movie, including a link to the trailer, which you can watch directly on your device, or select the list of theaters to go to the page that displays the exact showtimes.

Several other apps provide movie listings, including both WHERE and Yelp. However, none provides the amount of detailed information about the movie itself as IMDb.

CREATING SHOPPING LISTS

We all know the importance of using a list when shopping. Budgeting experts will tell you that you should have a list to avoid wasting money on impulse items, but the real reason is because you will likely forget something without one, and, of course, Murphy's Law says that whatever you forget will be an item that you simply cannot do without, forcing you to make a second trip.

Thankfully, quite a few apps exist on the Market to allow you to create a shopping list directly on your phone. My personal favorite is OI Shopping list. The OI in the name stands of Open Initiative; unlike most of the other apps on the Market, this one has been created by a group of people as an open-source application.

The application is incredibly simple, as a shopping list app should be. You can simply

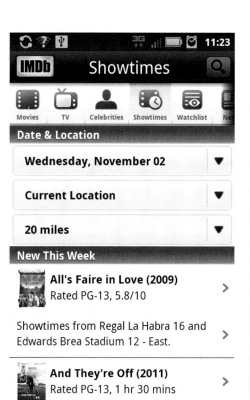

Figure 14.5

The IMDb app showing local movie listings

launch the app and begin entering products to create your list. While at the store, simply select the check mark next to each item as you pick it up to know that you have it in your cart (see Figure 14.6).

Press your phone's Menu button and select Clean up list to remove all checked items in preparation for your next trip to the store. You can also select Settings, then Sort order to change the way in which the items are sorted. I prefer the option unchecked first, alphabetical, which moves each item to the bottom of my list as I check it off.

If you prefer a bit more detail on your list, you can long-press an item and select Edit item to bring up a screen that allows you to enter quantity and price. You can also add tags to items, so, for example, you can tag milk and eggs as dairy, while you tag pineapple and grapes as fruit. You can then sort on these tags to see items that are likely to be close to each other in the store.

The app remembers any item you add, and presents you with an autocomplete option as you type new items, so the next time you need to get eggs, you should only need to type "e" and then select eggs from the list that appears.

The app also supports a few cool optional add-ons, the best of which is the OI Barcode Scanner, which allows you to scan the barcode on a product to add it to your list.

CALCULATING TIPS

Occasionally, restaurants will print suggested tips directly on the bill, but most of the time you are expected to calculate the gratuity in your head. I suppose some people are naturally good enough at math to be able to do so in their heads, but for most of us, you can get a rough approximation of 15 percent, but nothing more. While you could use the calculator that comes built in with Android, a dedicated tip calculator makes things easier.

Tip calculators are another popular category for apps. A recent search on Tip

Figure 14.6

OI Shopping list in action

Calculator brings up almost 1,000 apps, ranging from free to several dollars. Perhaps the most popular is TipCalculator by Trade-Fields (see Figure 14.7).

This app is nice because of its sheer simplicity. You set the tip amount at the top, and then enter the bill amount using the keypad at the bottom. Both the tip and the total bill appear back at the top. You can change the tax amount and split the bill between multiple people as well.

TAKING NOTES WITH EVERNOTE

I was first introduced to Evernote while attending a conference when a woman next to me noted I was taking notes in Word and recommended that I try Evernote instead. At that time, Evernote existed as an online service and a desktop application. The idea is that you can take notes with the desktop application, but that those notes are automatically synchronized online, giving you access to them from any other web-based computer. I tried it out at the conference and was quickly convinced as to its utility.

I love the ability to access notes from anywhere, and I use Evernote for all kinds of things: frequent flyer numbers, lists of the movies I have seen or books I have read, Wi-Fi access codes, people who help me out while I write books and need to be thanked in the acknowledgments, and more. The only thing missing for some time was the ability to get all of this on my phone. Yes, I could access the Evernote website, but it tended to be pretty slow on the phone and was not easy to read. I was thus thrilled when Evernote finally released an app for Android.

Figure 14.7
The TipCalculator

In order to use Evernote, you first need to sign up for an account. The company offers both a free account and a paid account that gives you additional storage space online. You can sign up online or within the app. When you log in, you are given six options to get started: You can create a new note, take a picture to be saved as a note, view all of your notes, view your tags, open your notebooks, or view shared notebooks (see Figure 14.8). You can also search for an existing note pressing the Search button at the top of the screen. The desktop and web versions of Evernote

rely heavily on tags to organize your notes. In the mobile app, tags can be considered in searching, but are not as obviously used elsewhere. Evernote also provides two home screen widgets: a small one that simply contains buttons to access the app, and a large one that displays your three most recently edited notes.

PLANNING TRIPS WITH KAYAK

I do a lot of traveling for work and needed an app that would allow me to keep travel arrangements organized. In particular, I hoped to find an app that would present me with a single location that I could use to look up flight details, rental car reservation numbers, and hotel addresses. This is again a category of apps that is fairly common on the Market, and something again that I evaluated a variety of apps without discovering any one that suited my needs. That is, until a friend recommended Kayak.

I was familiar with Kayak as a flight search tool: You can visit the website, enter your home and destination cities, and get a list of the cheapest flights between them. However, until I checked out the mobile app, I had never looked at the rest of the features the company offers. Now I use Kayak not only to find flights but also keep myself organized while traveling.

When you open the app you are presented with a set of options, allowing you to search flights or for hotels or rental cars (see Figure 14.9). I have used the flight search on occasion, but generally find the full web interface to be a lot easier to use, although I can imagine a situation where I might use it for an emergency.

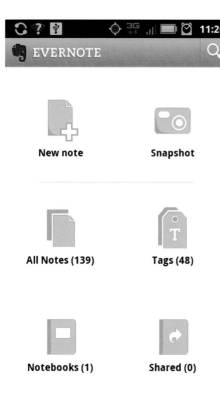

Figure 14.8

The Evernote app

What I find particularly nice is Kayak's Trip feature, which is the travel organization tool I was looking for. Once you create a free account with Kayak, you can store your flight, hotel, and rental car information on its servers, accessing the details from the web or within the application. What is really cool, though, is that you do not need to manually enter any of these details. Today, just about every travel-related business will e-mail you purchase confirmation receipts. All you need to do is forward these e-mails to trips@kayak.com and within a few minutes, the details will appear in your trip. The

service is intelligent enough to group related details together into a single trip, even if you send receipts separately.

KEEPING TRACK OF THE WEATHER WITH WEATHERBUG

I am not a weather geek. Most of the time, I have a vague idea that it is hot or cold outside. However, there are plenty of times when it helps to have a bit more information. It is not a good idea, for example, to let the kids go to school in T-shirts and shorts when it is going to be 50 degrees and raining. It helps when packing for a trip to have an idea of the weather where you are going.

WeatherBug is a great app whether you are like me and need some general info about the weather now and then or if you are a hard-core weather geek. When you launch the app, it will display local weather information: the current temperature, wind speed and direction, and today's high and low temperature (see Figure 14.10). It also displays today's forecast, along with the forecast for the next five days.

The app's real power is in its additional features. Along the bottom of the screen you will find a set of extra buttons. The first takes you to the main page and always displays the current temperature. The second button gives you a more detailed seven-day forecast; you can select any day to get more information. The third of the buttons at the bottom displays live weather radar for your area, while the fourth displays images from a variety of local weather cameras. The fifth and final button loads videos from the WeatherBug website, which give you weather information around the country.

You can press your phone's Menu button and select Location to add new locations to the app, helpful if you are traveling or just want to keep up to date on the weather someplace else. Also on the menu is an option for Preferences to change temperature displays to Celsius or to add the current temperature to your phone's Notifications Bar or tablet's Action bar.

RESEARCHING WITH WAPEDIA AND WIKIMOBILE

Several dozen apps exist that give you quick access to Wikipedia, not counting, of course, using the browser to simply access the website directly. The two that are fastest and most user friendly are Wapedia and Wikimobile.

Wapedia's interface is clean and easy to use, and the app tends to load articles quickly. Articles in Wapedia are laid out vertically, pretty much exactly as they are on the Wikipedia website, so you can quickly scroll through to find the information you need (see Figure 14.11). Press the phone's Menu button and then select the first option to jump to the article's contents. The title of the article displays the number of pages

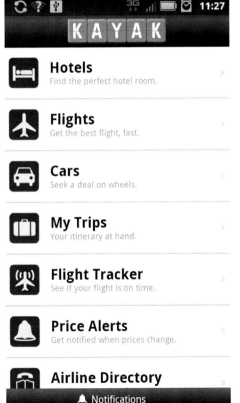

Figure 14.9
Kayak's main screen

Figure 14.10
WeatherBug's main page

the article contains, so you have a good idea at the beginning of how long the article is. Unfortunately, there is no easy way to get to the additional pages without first scrolling to the bottom of the current page, but besides that Wapedia is an excellent app.

Wikimobile is another excellent app for accessing Wikipedia. Articles load as pages that you read left to right, which can often be an easier way to read but unfortunately means that you occasionally have to wait a moment while the next set of pages loads. The good news is that you get to watch the app's cute dog-chasing-its-tail animation, so all is not lost. The app does not load images from the article by default — a big part of why articles load quickly — but you can use the phone's Menu button to turn on the option to load images if you want. Unlike Wapedia, Wikimobile also does not attempt to remember the last page you viewed.

FINDING RECIPES

I am always on the lookout for new recipes, and the Favorite Recipes app is a great way to discover new things to cook for dinner. The app has dozens of categories, and its search feature brings up a random selection of recipes for each matching phrase. There are no pictures accompanying the recipes, but the directions are laid out nicely and best of all, each of the recipes I have tried from the app has been very good.

For recipes of a different sort, check out Cocktail Hero. While not an exhaustive cocktail library — it says it contains 260 recipes — its best feature is its "Make It Mode," where you can check off the items you have in your liquor cabinet and it will tell you what cocktails you can make from those.

FOLLOWING YOUR FAVORITE SPORTS TEAMS

If you are a sports fan, you can use your phone to keep up with your favorite teams. It is no real surprise that the best free app for tracking sports scores comes from none other than ESPN. Its ScoreCenter app displays a wealth of information about ongoing and past games. You can set favorite teams in baseball, basketball, cricket, football, ice hockey, rugby, and soccer, and have access to all of the major leagues within each sport. The app defaults to showing you the scores

Battle of Agincourt (1/6)

The **Battle of Agincourt**[a] was a major English victory against a numerically superior French army in the Hundred Years' War. The battle occurred on Friday, 25 October 1415 (Saint Crispin's Day), near modern-day Azincourt, in northern France. [6] [b]Henry V's victory crippled France and started a new period in the war, during which Henry married the French king's daughter and his son, Henry VI, was made heir to the throne of France (although Henry VI failed to capitalize on his father's battlefield success).

Henry V led his troops into battle and participated in hand-to-hand fighting.

Figure 14.11

Wapedia accessing the Wikipedia article on Android

and information for these favorites, so you get the information you want quickly without having to wade through a bunch of data you do not need or care about.

My favorite feature of this app is its home screen widget, which displays the upcoming game for each of your favorite teams. You can scroll through your teams using the small arrows to the left of the widget, and each team's next game displays at the bottom. While a game is in progress, the widget automatically updates to display the current score.

If you are a baseball fan, you simply need MLB At Bat, the official app provided by Major League Baseball. The app allows you to customize it to set your favorite team, and includes a home screen widget that automatically displays today's score for that team. The app also allows you to listen to any radio broadcast of any Major League baseball game, a great feature if you are on the road and cannot get your local team's broadcast. Perhaps its coolest feature, however, is Gameday, which provides a live, pitch-by-pitch view of any game in progress (see Figure 14.12). It isn't quite as good as watching a game live or on TV, but it is certainly an effective way to follow a game if you cannot make it to the ballpark or you are not near a TV. A new version is released every year. At the beginning of the season, it runs $14.95, but is gradually discounted as the season progresses, so if you only care about the World Series you can buy it in October for around $1.

SCANNING BARCODES

You can use your phone's camera to scan barcodes on a variety of products. A wide variety of applications can use this data to show you details on the product.

QR codes, once the domain of websites wanting to provide scannable links to download apps, are now popping up everywhere: on billboards, business cards, in books, and of course still on the web. All of these can be scanned with Barcode Scanner by ZXing Team. You can also scan the barcode on the backs of books and many other products, which you can then use to search the web for details on the product.

P: Carpenter 2.95 (81 pitches, 46S, 35B)
AB: Beltre, A 0-2, .310 **Deck:** Cruz, N

1. Adrian Beltre grounds out, pitcher Chris Carpenter to first baseman Albert Pujols.
Pitch 3 In play, out(s) (85.0 mph Cutter)
Pitch 2 Called Strike (86.0 mph Cutter)
Pitch 1 Called Strike (86.1 mph Cutter)

Figure 14.12

The Gameday feature of the MLB At Bat app, showing game 7 of the 2011 World Series

207

This is an app that should be on everyone's device.

Another app that uses the camera to scan barcodes is Amazon's app. When you launch the app, you have an option from the main screen to search using barcodes. When a barcode is recognized as being from a product Amazon sells, the company's detail page about the product will display (see Figure 14.13). You can purchase the product immediately from Amazon from here, or, the way I more frequently use it, you can add the product to your Amazon wish list in the hope that someone else buys it for you.

Key Ring is yet another great app that relies on scanning barcodes. This ingenious app lets you scan the barcodes on customer loyalty cards. It then saves a high-resolution picture of the barcode from the card. You can then stop carrying the actual card, and instead have the clerk at the store scan your phone. You need to be sure that your phone's screen is clean, but most of the time this will work without issue. The app does display the membership number on-screen, so if scanning does not work the number will be there for the clerk to type in manually, ensuring that you still get credit for your purchase.

TRANSLATING WITH GOOGLE TRANSLATE

Science fiction has long had solutions that allow characters to communicate with others who speak different languages, from *Star Trek*'s Universal Translator or *The Hitchhiker's Guide to the Galaxy*'s Babel fish. While it does not yet know Klingon, the Google Translate app brings you close to making this fiction reality.

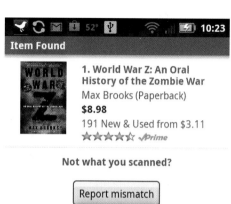

Figure 14.13

Amazon's detail page, generated from scanning barcodes on the books

When you open Google Translate, you can enter a word or phrase and select to translate to and from any of 53 languages. The app will display the word in the chosen language, but what is particularly cool is its ability to actually speak the word by selecting the speaker icon (see Figure 14.14). In order to use the spoken translation, you need to have the Text-to-speech Extended app installed as well. Fortunately, Google Translate will automatically prompt you to install Text-to-speech when you first launch if it is not already installed.

SEARCHING WITH GESTURE SEARCH

Google, quite obviously, offers a number of Android apps. There are common ones such as Gmail and Docs and specialized ones like Translate and Sky Maps. Gesture Search, however, is my personal favorite, and I am always a bit surprised by how few people seem to know about this phenomenally useful app.

The app is quite simple: When you open it, are you given a basically blank screen. What you need to do is start writing whatever you are searching for by simply drawing letters on the screen. As you spell a word, the app will automatically begin presenting you with items that match, searching your contact list, web browser favorites, phone settings, and most usefully, your apps (see Figure 14.15). As soon as you have spelled enough of the word to get whatever you are searching for to appear, simply select it. If you choose a contact, that person's contact page will open so you can quickly call, send a text, or look up the address. Selecting a web favorite will, of course, launch that page in your browser, while choosing an app launches the app.

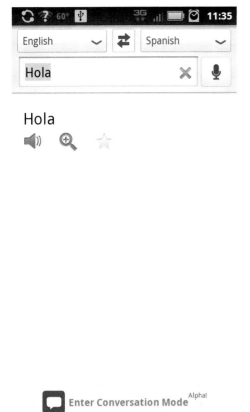

Figure 14.14
Google Translate

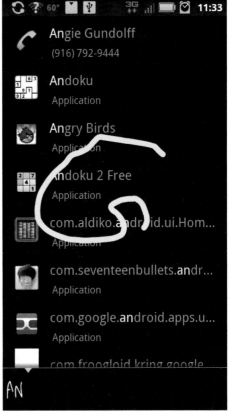

Figure 14.15
Gesture Search

If you make a mistake and add a letter you did not mean to, simply draw a straight line from the right edge of the screen to the left; you can clear your current word entirely by dragging a line from the left edge to the right in the bottom section of the screen that shows what you have written so far.

I have Gesture Search on my main home screen, and it is easily the app I use the most. I hardly ever access my Applications Bin, because any app I want to open I can find more easily with Gesture Search. The same applies to the Contacts app. Like all other Google apps, Gesture Search is free.

GETTING NEWS WITH PULSE

While many news organizations provide apps, Pulse allows you to get your news from a huge variety of sources. The free app displays a list of news sources with a few of their major headlines (see Figure 14.16). The sources that are displayed and the order they display are fully customizable by clicking the gear icon in the top-left corner of the screen. The app allows you to scroll both up and down to view your sources and, within a source, left and right to view more headlines. Simply select the headline of any article you wish to view to see the opening sentence of the article and a link to the original article on the source's website.

TAKING CREDIT CARDS WITH SQUARE

Square is one of those apps that is guaranteed to make people do a double-take when they see you use it. The app is free and available from the Market. When you download it and launch it the first time, you go through a simple registration process to

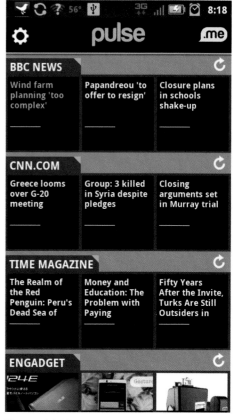

Figure 14.16

Pulse

establish an account. You will also be asked for a mailing address, and here is the really cool part: In about a week, you will receive a nifty little device in the mail. About the size of a quarter, the device plugs into your phone or tablet's headphone jack and serves as a credit card reader (see Figure 14.17). After that, you are all set to start accepting credit cards: Simply swipe the card through the reader. Enter the amount of the transaction, and then hand your phone or tablet to your customer. Using their finger, they sign right on your device, and you are done. Later that evening, check your bank balance on

Figure 14.17
The Square credit card reader plugged into my phone

the street. He told them he was a starving art student, and could they help? When they tried to brush him off with the normal "sorry, no cash", he looked at them and said, "That's okay. I take plastic." It was really nothing more than a social experiment, but enough people were intrigued by it that he ended up making about $50.

your bank's website or, if your bank offers one, its app and you will see the amount of your credit card transaction, minus a 2.75% processing fee charged by Square.

Pretty impressive. I got mine mostly because I think it is pretty cool, but I can actually come up with a bunch of ways to potentially use it. As an independent consultant, I can now accept credit cards as payment for my services. Taking the kids around the neighborhood to do Scout or school fundraising? If you have a neighbor who wants to buy whatever your kids are selling but doesn't have the cash? No problem. You now take credit cards. One student of mine — and I do not recommend this, but have to give him credit for creativity — got Square and went out to our downtown area and randomly approached people on

15

Troubleshooting

The Skim

While there are a lot of great things about modern mobile devices, one disputable issue is that they are, in the end, computers, and just like every other computer, they will occasionally run into problems. Most of the time, the issues can be best solved by rebooting your device, but in some cases more steps may be required.

KILLING APPS

Before I discuss how to kill a misbehaving app, I want to take a moment and discuss when not to kill an app. Applications that exist to kill other applications — called task killers — have been a staple of the Android market practically from its inception, and I cannot tell how many of my friends, upon first getting an Android device, ask me which one is best. My answer is always the same: none of them.

The perceived need for a task killer comes from two things: first, the lack of any obvious way to stop or close most apps, and second, a fundamental misunderstanding of how apps work and how Android manages apps in the first place. The first issue — the fact that very few apps have a built-in way to close themselves — derives from app developers, mostly, understanding the reality of the second issue, so that is the better place to start. Once you understand how Android handles apps in the first place, you will understand why apps are not developed with a "close" button and why task killers are not necessary.

The first, fundamental thing to understand here is that the Android operating system is fundamentally different from the Windows and Macintosh systems. However, since almost everyone grew up and learned on one or both of those systems, there is a not-unreasonable assumption that Android is just like them, but smaller. In fact, there are a lot of very key differences between how a desktop operating system and a mobile operating system can and should work, but for our purposes here the only one to really understand is memory management.

A word of caution before we get started: While I will do my best to minimize it, the next few paragraphs necessarily contain a lot of pretty technical information. If you would rather not read it and are willing instead to just take my word for it that app killers are not really needed, then go ahead and skip down to the next heading.

Both your desktop or laptop computer and your mobile device contain a kind of temporary memory called RAM. When you boot up your computer, the operating system loads itself into RAM. Other programs that you use all the time, such as an instant messenger, might load as well. Your device does the same thing: When you boot it, Android loads into RAM. In both cases, the device is then going to try to fill up the remaining RAM with whatever it can— namely, applications. Every time you launch a program on your computer or an app on your device, that program or app opens into your machine's RAM, and it stays there until told otherwise.

Freeing up RAM is where your desktop operating system and your mobile operating system differ. Desktop operating systems give you the user total control over what is running and what is not. As I write this, I have Microsoft Word, Mozilla Firefox, and the Android SDK running on my laptop, as I need all three in order to compose this. I also have a music program running, because like all other authors I know I like to write to music. As soon as I am done writing, I will close Word, freeing up the portion of my system's RAM currently being used by Word. There is basically no other way for me to regain that space: If I need to open a particularly memory-intensive application, I must manually close other programs first. Otherwise, the computer will run out of RAM and then everything will slow to a crawl.

Android, on the other hand, manages its memory internally. As I mentioned earlier, a certain portion of your device's RAM is taken up all the time by Android itself. The rest is taken up by the apps you run. But here, Android is in many ways smarter than the Windows or MacOS. Instead of filling up available RAM until it runs out, and then slowing everything down by trying to load more programs on top of that, Android looks at the available RAM every time you launch a new app. If there is some open space, which will generally only happen immediately after you boot the phone, the app simply loads. More often, though, all of your RAM is already full, so Android knows that in order to load that new app, it needs to close something else, and it does that. It is not a simply first in, first out rule, though. Rather, the operating system is paying attention to what you are doing (but not in a creepy Big Brother way) and it knows that you have, for example, been using

Gmail and Tweetdeck and Angry Birds a lot, so it is not going to close those, but will instead close some of those apps that you opened briefly and have not gone back to. Thus, if you consider that the only real reason you ever need to close an app is to free up memory for other apps, you can see that manually closing apps on your device is not as important as closing apps on your laptop.

Where things get confusing is that Android does make this obvious. Instead, it makes it look like apps run all the time. In Gingerbread, you can long-press on your Home button to see the list of recent apps. This shows all of the apps you have opened since you last rebooted, and you can easily select any of them to return to it. Honeycomb shows a similar list when you select the multitasking button in the bottom-left corner of the screen. This leads many to reach the not-illogical conclusion that all of these apps are running all the time. Because we also know that some apps can present a considerable drain on the battery, you can understand why users might want some way to close an app. But you have to understand that what you see there is not a list of running apps, but rather it is exactly what it says: a list of recent apps. Some of them may very well be running, but not all.

One more thing: Even if an app is still running in the background, it most likely is not using all of its services, and so therefore it may not be presenting a drain on the battery. Maps is a good example. Maps, because it uses GPS, can drain your battery very quickly. However, it only uses GPS when it is the current, active app. When you switch to another app on your device, Maps will continue to run so long as the system does not decide it needs its memory, but it will turn

off GPS. You can actually see this: Launch Maps, and note that the GPS icon appears in the Notifications Bar. Then switch to some other app by simply pressing the Home button and launching something else. Maps will almost certainly continue to run, but the GPS icon will turn off, which you can tell because the icon will disappear.

The next question that comes up in all of this is what happens if an application is actively tracking data while you use it, but then you switch to something else and Android decides to close that program to free up space before you get back to it. A simple example is a game: If you are in the middle of a level when, say, the phone rings, what happens to your in-progress game? Here, Google has left this to developers. The simple reality of creating an app for Android is that your application might get interrupted at any time, and your application may get closed by the system at any time. Therefore, developers need to plan for this. Any well-written application that needs to actively track data, as in our aforementioned game, needs to have a way to detect when it goes into the background and automatically save its data and provide a way to restore this data when the application launches again.

Force-stopping Apps

So you now hopefully have an understanding as to why task killer apps are not really needed most of the time in Android. (It is also possible that you skipped the section above and are just taking my word for it, which is also okay.) Why, then, do task killers exist at all? Are they all just bad apps waiting to trap unsuspecting users? The answer, in short, is no. There are a few legitimate reasons to work with one.

As mentioned previously, you do not need to manually close apps to free up space. In fact, manually closing an app in Android can have some negative consequences, and it is possible that the task you kill might be needed by some other task, or even the operating system itself, and closing it might cause instability.

That said, there are times when you might need to manually kill a task. The most obvious, and unfortunately frequent, reason is when an app locks up. Android is fairly good about warning you when an app is misbehaving. In many cases, you will get a warning that an app has locked up that offers to allow you to wait for the app or to force close it. Other times, though, you might want to not wait for the system to figure this out and instead just want to kill the app yourself.

Before you download something to do this, you should know that an app killer is built into Android. From your home screen, select the Menu button, then Settings. Next, select Applications, then Manage Applications. From here, the interface may vary a bit from one system to the next, but most will offer you screens from which you can select from apps you have downloaded, all apps, apps on your SD card, and running apps. If you do not have all of those choices or if the wording is a bit different, do not worry, as all you need to do is find the app, regardless of which tab it appears in (and most will appear in more than one tab anyway). So scroll down to the misbehaving app and select it. From the screen that appears, select Force stop (see Figure 15.1).

The only advantage of using a task killer app is that you can usually force close an app in fewer steps. Otherwise, they are merely doing something that the system does by

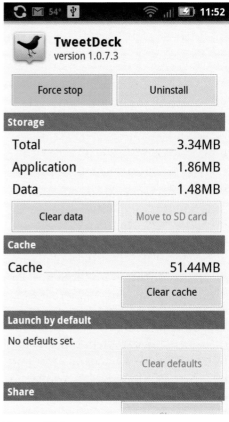

Figure 15.1
Manually forcing an app to close

itself. The problem is that lot of these apps do a lot more, and many times they can create huge problems on your phone. So, it is far better to just stick with the procedure the device provides. Yes, it will take a few extra steps, but in the end it is far safer.

FORCING A REBOOT

Like all computers, your device will at times lock up. This can happen for any number of reasons, but when it occurs understanding exactly why is not usually your priority; instead, you just need to get your device working again.

Every device provides some method to allow you to manually reboot. Most involve pressing two or three of the physical buttons on the device at the same time. On the Xoom, for instance, you can force a reboot by pressing the power button and the up volume button together. Phones have an added option for reboot: Simply open the back cover and pull out the battery, wait a few seconds, and then put it back in and turn the phone back on.

Your device should not need to be rebooted frequently. If it does, there is something much more serious going on. The normal culprit is a misbehaving app, but tracking it down can be time consuming to say the least: You need to uninstall your apps, one at a time, and use your device for a bit between each install until the problem goes away, at which point you can assume that the last app you uninstalled is the problem. The possibility of a hardware issue also exists, so fixing a frequent-reboot problem might involve a trip to the nearest physical location for your carrier.

FORMATTING YOUR SD CARD

Your SD card holds your music and stores videos and pictures you shoot with your device. It also possibly holds some of your apps. If it should fail, you will potentially lose a lot of valuable information. Thankfully, you will not lose your Google account information that identifies you to the device, since that is stored on the device itself, and you should not lose data like phone numbers and calendar events, since those are automatically and frequently synced with Google's servers.

In a worst-case scenario, if something goes wrong with your SD card, you may be able to restore it by reformatting it. Reformatting erases all of the data on the card and returns it to its fresh-out-of-the-box state, so if the problem with the card is corrupt data, a reformat should help.

You can reformat the card using your phone by going to the home screen, selecting the Menu button, choosing Settings, and then selecting Storage. From here, you will see an option to reformat your card (see Figure 15.2). If it is grayed out, you may need to first select the option above it to unmount your SD card. Once that is complete, you

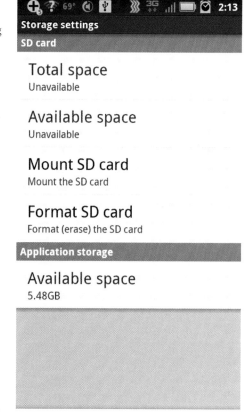

Figure 15.2
The option to format your SD card. Use with caution!

should be able to format. Be absolutely sure that you have backed up any important data on the card, as there is no way to undo a reformat.

You can also reformat the card using your computer, which might be your only option if the problems with the card are causing your device to become unstable. In order to do this, you will first need to remove the card from your device. Following the steps outlined previously, go into the Storage section of Settings and unmount your card. Then, carefully remove it from the device. On most phones, you will need to remove the battery cover and possibly the battery itself to access the card. If your card is causing errors such that you cannot access settings, you can simply remove the card without unmounting it, but you should only do this if you absolutely cannot unmount it.

In order to read the card on your computer, you will need an SD card reader. Almost every computer manufactured in the last several years has a card reader built in, but if yours does not you should be able to purchase one at any electronics store for around $10. You may also need an adapter, since your device uses a MicroSD card and many card readers only have a slot for a standard-size card. The good news here is that you most likely already have the adapter, as almost all MicroSD cards include one.

Once you have the right hardware, you can format the card by inserting it into the computer's card reader and waiting a moment for the computer to recognize it. If you use Windows, simply open Windows Explorer, right-click on the card, and select Format. Be sure to set the format to FAT32. On a Mac, you will need to go into Applica-

tions, then Utilities, and then open Disk Utility. From there, select the SD card and choose the Erase button from the screen. Make sure you choose FAT as the file format.

BOOTING INTO RECOVERY MODE

In some extreme cases — namely, if your phone will not boot up at all or if it gets itself into what is referred to online as a "boot loop," where it continually boots, shuts down, and reboots — you may need to go into Recovery mode on your phone. From here, you may be able to boot directly into the phone, or in a worst-case scenario, perform a factory reset.

The exact steps for booting into Recovery mode vary from phone to phone, so you will need to check online for the exact steps. On the Droid X, for example, you can power off the phone, then hold both the Home and Power buttons down until the Motorola logo appears. At that point, let go of the Power button but continue holding down the Home button until you see an exclamation mark and the Android robot. Once there, release Home and press the Search button once, which takes you into Recovery mode. (If the phone gets stuck on the screen with the exclamation mark, press both volume keys at the same time to get past it.) On the Xoom, you enter Recovery mode by pressing the Power button, waiting until you see the Motorola Dual Core screen, and then pressing the Volume Down key repeatedly until you are given an "Android Recovery" option.

Recovery mode does not have the pretty interface that you are used to in Android. Instead, you are essentially working in the Unix-based underpinnings of the system, so you will need to rely entirely on menus. On most devices, you can use the Volume keys to navigate within Recovery mode, but again this might vary from device to device to check online if that does not work.

You may have three or four choices once in Recovery mode, but the two important ones are the reboot the system and apply a factory reset. Rebooting your system will often solve boot loop issues, so it is probably the option you should try first. If that fails, return to Recovery mode and select Factory Reset. Be aware, however, that a factory reset restores your device to its out-of-the-box settings, so you will have to start over, including signing in to the device with your Google username and password, reapplying any and all customizations such as ringtones and home screen wallpapers and shortcuts, and most annoyingly reinstalling all of your applications. Officially, Android 2.2 and later will automatically download and install all of your applications, but I have only had that happen a couple of times when I have done a factory reset. Most often, I end up having to download everything manually. Apps you have installed from the Amazon Appstore or other sources will never reinstall automatically.

ROOTING

No guide to Android would be complete without at least some discussion of rooting your device. When you get an Android device, you are running the Android system under a somewhat limited user account. Primarily, the limits on the account are transparent to the user, so you will not generally encounter permission errors that you might see trying to navigate a corporate network. Most of the limits protect both you and the

phone by restricting the sorts of things apps can do on the system, but in some cases, the limits also help protect the revenue stream of your carrier. A great example of this is tethering: using your device's data connection to set up a Wi-Fi hotspot to allow computers to get online. Android, by itself, supports tethering, but carriers such as Verizon want to sell you a monthly service for this feature, so Verizon devices limit access to the tethering functionality of Android, thus forcing its users to pay for the service. Also, a continual and continuing issue with many Android users is the time delay between the release of a new version of Android and their carrier deciding to provide that release to its users. In most cases, rooted users can upgrade to newer versions of Android much more quickly.

Rooting gets you around these issues. As was mentioned earlier in this chapter, Android is built on top of the Unix operating system. In a Unix environment, the so-called "super user" — the user account with

TIP

If your device does not automatically redownload and reinstall all of your applications, use a computer to go online and browse to http://market.android.com. The Market app on your device will not likely remember all of your apps, but the Market website will. You can simply select the My Library link, then click each app and select Install. This will push the app to your device and install it.

unlimited access to everything on the system — is known as "root." When you root your device, you are essentially upgrading your user account to the super-user level, giving you complete access to everything on the phone, including features like carrier-free tethering.

I cannot outline the steps to root your device here, as they vary greatly from one device to another. Also, no carrier directly supports or endorses rooting; instead, users in the Android community provide the resources to do it. This brings two implications: First, you cannot call your carrier's customer service department or take your device to a local carrier store for trouble-shooting if you root; and second, there is always a time delay between the release of a new product and the release of instructions on how to root it. Therefore, if you purchase the newest and greatest phone or tablet as soon as it is released, you will have to wait before someone figures out how to root.

You can find the instructions for rooting your device by going to Google and searching for your device name and the word root; for example, a Google search for "Droid X root" finds thousands of results. In general, rooting will involve downloading files from a website, copying them to your SD card, and then booting into Recovery mode. From there, you will usually launch the files you downloaded. In some cases, you might also have to purchase and download an app from the Market.

Along the process of rooting, your device will undergo a factory reset, so be sure to back up any important data. Be prepared to spend some time rooting, as it usually takes one or two hours. Finally, be sure that your device is fully charged before you begin the process, as you will usually not be able to plug it in while rooting is taking place.

Rooting can greatly enhance your experience using your device, but should be undertaken with caution. In most cases, mistakes during the rooting process will require that you perform a normal factory reset and then start over, but the possibility of rendering your device useless, known colloquially as "bricking" the device, is not out of the question. Be careful!

16

Advanced Topics

The Skim

For most users, understanding how to work your phone, take pictures, and install and run apps will be enough. Others, however, will want to do more. You can fine-tune your phone's power settings to get more time between charges, or use your phone to get your computer online. With the Android Software Development Kit, you can back up applications and take screenshots. You can also create your own apps.

MANAGING YOUR PHONE'S POWER SETTINGS

Battery life has gotten significantly better on the latest generation of smartphones, and it will presumably continue to improve. That said, no one can deny that smartphones will drain their battery far faster than a normal mobile phone. While a non-smartphone user can go days or even weeks between charges, you will likely need to plan to keep your smartphone plugged in as much as you can; most cannot go for more than a day or two between charges, and if you use things like GPS or the camera, you will get much less than that.

A variety of apps exists to help you improve battery life. On some phones, Android will include a battery manager application by default in the phone's settings, accessible by pressing the Menu button from the home screen.

The Battery Manager allows you to choose between viewing battery usage or setting a battery mode. The battery usage displays a list of the applications you have running and how much of your battery they are consuming (see Figure 16.1). The battery modes let you fine-tune your battery usage. Three modes exist by default: a Maximum battery saver that stops synching data after 15 minutes regardless of the time and dims the display, a Nighttime saver that stops synching at night but leaves data sync on during the day and does not affect the display brightness, and Performance mode, which leaves all settings alone and in essence does nothing to preserve the battery.

You can also set up a custom mode, where you can define exactly what hours should have automatic synching, how long the phone should wait until it stops synching, and your desired display brightness.

If your version of Android does not include battery management tools, you can download one of the many power management apps from the Market, such as Power Manager from X-Phone Software. The free version of the app has a set of profiles preconfigured to progressively dim the screen as power gets lower. It would also begin to disable features such as GPS when the power reaches a certain threshold. The commercial version of the application, which only costs $.99, allows you to configure your own profiles.

You can also help manage power by paying attention to GPS and Wi-Fi settings, both of which can drain your power. Most apps that require GPS will automatically turn it off as soon as you leave the app,

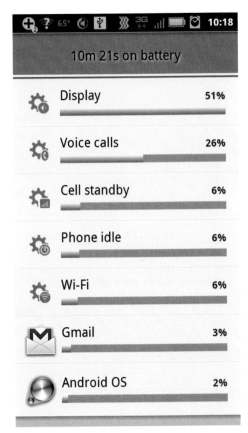

Figure 16.1

Apps currently using up my battery

either to return to the home screen or go to a different app, but if you ever notice that the GPS indicator is showing on the Notifications Bar when no app is open that should be using it, you should be aware that you may be draining your power unnecessarily. Keep in mind that some apps, such as Navigate, will keep running, and keep using GPS, even in the background.

I use Wi-Fi on my phone all the time when I am home, as it is almost always faster than a 3G connection, but then I also have my phone plugged in, either to the wall or, more likely, the computer when I am home. Wi-Fi is another power-hungry service, so if you cannot keep your phone plugged in most of the time, you might think about not using it.

GET YOUR COMPUTER ONLINE WITH YOUR PHONE

A recent sit-com episode revolved around a character who had moved in with his father. The son, a writer, needed to be online, but the older father did not see the need for the Internet. I can fully relate with the son — I hate having to be off-line. Unfortunately, I still encounter situations where I cannot get online easily. I sometimes teach at facilities that, for security purposes, do not allow me to connect to their network and do not have guest Wi-Fi networks. Incredibly, I even teach regularly at a technology school with no Wi-Fi. As a traveler, it has been a long time since I have been at a hotel that does not provide Internet service, but many hotels charge exorbitant fees to get online, and most hotel networks are painfully slow.

Fortunately, you can now get your computer online with your phone or tablet with a data connection using a variety of methods. The first official method is to use the Verizon Hotspot utility. Obviously, this only works if you have a phone running on Verizon's network, and even then Verizon does not support it on all of its phones. For those phones that are supported, it is a very easy process: Simply launch the Mobile Hotspot tool that came preinstalled on your phone, agree to the terms of service, and connect. The downside to this method is its cost: Verizon currently charges $20 per month on top of your existing service charges. The big advantage is that this turns your phone into a true mobile

hotspot, so other machines besides yours can connect as well if you allow them. Other carriers offer similar services along the lines of Verizon's, and likewise vary based on which phones they support and how much they charge, but an additional monthly charge is the industry standard.

Fortunately, there are several free alternatives. If you have a laptop with a Bluetooth connection, you may be able to connect your computer to your device via Bluetooth and then use the device's data connection to get your computer online. The exact steps necessary to enable connecting via Bluetooth vary greatly depending on your device, your version of Android, and your laptop's operating system, but if it can be done with your combination of hardware and software, you should be able to find details online. Bluetooth tethering is the method I use most often if I just need to get online quickly, such as a recent incident when I needed to download an e-mail attachment onto my laptop but was sitting in an airport with no free Wi-Fi. Bluetooth is a quick and easy way to connect, but it will generally be quite slow and I have found it usually renders my phone all but useless while it is connected.

PDANet, an app available in the Market, provides another alternative. The app is very simple to use. Install it on your device, and then install a companion piece of software on your laptop, available from www.junefabrics.com/android/. Once both programs are installed, you can plug your device into your computer via USB, then enable sharing in the app on your device. Finally, turn on the connection by simply clicking the Connect link in the program on your computer and you will be online.

PDANet is available in a free version that provides a fully featured trial, after which the app blocks connections to secure websites but continues to work on nonsecure sites. The full version, which allows connections to secure sites, is available for purchase.

Another alternative is Proxoid, which sets your device up as a proxy server for your computer. Proxoid is free, but requires a considerable amount of setup on your computer, all of which will need to be undone when you return to a normal connection. Thus, it can be helpful for long trips but is impractical if you need to frequently switch between having your computer connected to home or work and connecting via your device. Prox-

oid is available in the Market, while details on the necessary setup on your computer are at http://code.google.com/p/proxoid/. Using Proxoid also requires that you have the Android SDK installed; see the following section for details.

Many other options exist to allow tethering, but most all require that you have root access to your device. As the steps required to root your device vary wildly from one model to the next, it is not covered expressly in this book, but many resources exist online to step you through the process.

DOWNLOADING THE ANDROID SDK

A Software Development Kit, or SDK, is a package of tools provided by the developer of the language for programmers to use when creating applications. The Android SDK can be downloaded for free from Google at http://developer.android.com/sdk/index.html (see Figure 16.2). Even if you do not plan to build Android apps, having the SDK installed on your computer allows you to do a variety of other things such as take screenshots of your device and manually back up its data.

After you download the SDK, unzip it into a folder of your choosing on your computer. Then open the folder and double-click the SDK Setup file. If you want to install the complete SDK, which will allow you to have its full functionality, select Accept All on the Choose Packages to Install screen, then click Install Accepted. Be aware that this might take a while — I have a fast Internet connection and a fast machine, and this installation took about 15 minutes.

After you have the SDK installed, you will also need to install the Java SDK, also

TIDBIT

All of the images from the phone in this book were captured by copying and pasting. I use Adobe Photoshop, which has a very handy feature whereby if an image exists on the clipboard, selecting File, then New automatically creates a new document that is the size of whatever is on the clipboard. Images from the Debug Monitor will be at your phone's native resolution; for the Droid X, that is 854 × 480 pixels, while the Xoom is at 1280 × 800. I did not manipulate the image in any way in Photoshop; instead, I was using it simply to get the images into the TIFF file format requested by the publisher. I actually created an action in Photoshop to further simplify this process. If you are interested in reading more about how I did this, you can read about it on my blog at www.robhuddleston.com.

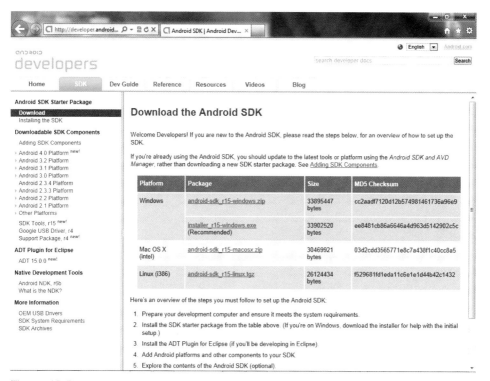

Figure 16.2

The Android SDK page

known as the JDK. Java is the language on which Android is built, so you cannot do much without it. Visit www.oracle.com/technetwork/java/javase/downloads/index.html and download whichever the most current version of the JDK is.

TURNING ON USB DEBUGGING

In order for your device to communicate with the tools in the SDK, you will need to enable USB Debugging. This is a very simple process: On your device, simply go to the home screen, then press the Menu button and select Settings. In Settings, select Applications, then Development, then select USB Debugging. You will get a warning message about how debugging is only for development purposes; select OK. You will now see an extra indicator on your Notifications Bar. In Android 2.2, this is the Android mascot with extra legs so that it looks like a bug, while on Honeycomb it is the mascot looking like a bee.

Your next step in getting your device set up with the SDK is the part that I had the most troubles with, and from reading online forums I was clearly not alone. You need to have the proper drivers installed in order for your device to fully communicate with the SDK. Hopefully, as soon as you plug your phone into your computer, it will detect the device and display a notification about finding drivers. The operating system should fail to find the right drivers, so it should ask you to manually install them, which you can do by going into the usb_driver folder in the SDK.

When I first attempted to do this with the Droid X on Windows 7, it did not work, and eventually I needed to go download new Droid X drivers online. After upgrading to Android 2.2, I again ran into problems, which I eventually worked around by turning USB Debugging off when I need the device in PC Mode and turning it back on when I need to work in USB Mass Storage mode. I encountered similar problems getting the Xoom working initially; in the end, downloading new drivers seemed to do the trick.

TAKING SCREENSHOTS

I initially thought that taking screenshots of your Android screen would be of very little interest outside of authors and bloggers. I was therefore surprised by how often it comes up on forums and even in people asking me how to do it. I am not sure exactly why so many people want to do it, but fortunately once you get the setup done it is a fairly easy process.

The simplest method of doing screenshots is via the oddly named Dalvik Debug Monitor, one of the tools in the SDK. Once you have the SDK installed and all of the proper drivers working, you can launch the monitor by going into the folder into which you unzipped the SDK, opening the tools

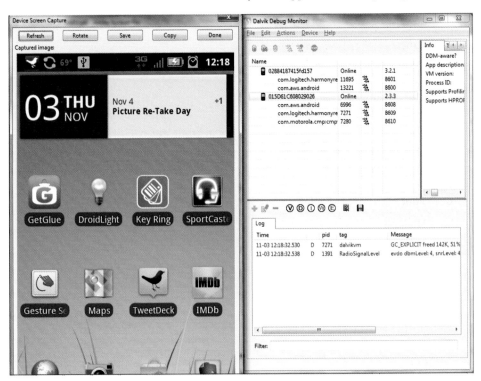

Figure 16.3
Capturing an image off the phone

folder, and double-clicking ddms.bat. This
tool will open to the Dalvik Debug Monitor,
which will show your device. If your device
does not show up, go back and ensure that
the proper drivers are installed. Also, make
sure that your device has USB Debugging
enabled.

If you interact with your phone while
plugged into the monitor, you can see a
fairly constant set of information scrolling
across the bottom. Everything happening on your phone is being monitored and
reported, which is useful for developers but
mostly unintelligible to everyone else.

When you are in the monitor, select
Device, then Screen Capture. This will open
a second screen, which after a moment
should display your device (see Figure 16.3).
This is a static picture of your device; if you
change anything on the device, you will
need to press the Refresh button to update
the image.

From here, you can click Save to save the
image to your hard drive in the PNG format.
If you need higher-quality images or require
other formats, you can instead click Copy
to place the image on your clipboard. Then
you can open an image-editing tool such
as Adobe Photoshop, paste the image, and
work with it from there.

Index

•URLs•